THE HAMLYN LECTURES
THIRTY-FIFTH SERIES

HAMLYN REVISITED

THE BRITISH LEGAL SYSTEM
TODAY

AUSTRALIA
Law Book Company Ltd.
Sydney : Melbourne : Brisbane

CANADA and U.S.A.
The Carswell Company Ltd.
Agincourt, Ontario

INDIA
N. M. Tripathi Private Ltd.
Bombay
and
Eastern Law House Private Ltd.
Calcutta *and* Delhi
M. P. P. House, Bangalore

ISRAEL
Steimatzky's Agency Ltd.
Jerusalem : Tel Aviv : Haifa

MALAYSIA : SINGAPORE : BRUNEI
Malayan Law Journal (Pte.) Ltd.
Singapore

NEW ZEALAND
Sweet & Maxwell (N.Z.) Ltd.
Auckland

PAKISTAN
Pakistan Law House
Karachi

HAMLYN REVISITED

THE BRITISH LEGAL SYSTEM TODAY

by

**LORD HAILSHAM
OF ST. MARYLEBONE**
C.H., F.R.S., D.C.L.

Published under the auspices of
THE HAMLYN TRUST

LONDON
STEVENS & SONS
1983

Published in 1983
by Stevens & Sons Limited of
11 New Fetter Lane, London
Printed in Great Britain
by Page Bros. (Norwich) Ltd.

British Library Cataloguing in Publication Data
Hailsham of St. Marylebone, Quinton Hogg,
Baron
Hamlyn revisited.—(The Hamlyn
Lectures; 35th series)
1. Justice, Administration of—
Great Britain
I. Title   II. Series
344.107   KD654

ISBN 0-420-46720-3
ISBN 0-420-46730-0 Pbk

©
Lord Hailsham of St. Marylebone
1983

CONTENTS

Contents

THE HAMLYN LECTURES

THE HAMLYN TRUST

EMMA WARBURTON HAMLYN was born in Devon on November 5, 1860 at Tormoham, now part of Torquay, the daughter of William Bussell Hamlyn and the former Emma Gorsuch Warburton. At the time of her birth her father described himself as a law clerk. He was admitted a solicitor 16 years later in May 1877 and practised, first in Newton Abbott and then in Torquay, until shortly before the First World War. He sat as a Justice of the Peace for some years. The family claimed to trace its lineage back to the Conquest.

Miss Hamlyn, who never married, is said to have studied law, though with what degree of industry is not recorded. She travelled widely. She was well-versed in literature, music and art and was a frequent visitor to Europe and the Mediterranean. She was particularly interested in comparative jurisprudence and in the relationship between the law and the culture of a people. She came to be a great admirer of the law and institutions of her own country.

A cousin later recalled her as an Edwardian lady, wearing long dark dresses and "large, dark hats with semi-herbaceous borders for trimming." She was "quite a character," "autocratic rather than otherwise," and "very intellectual." When she came to make her will on June 12, 1939 she insisted that her own draft of the gift of residue be adopted without amendment. She died at home in Torquay on September 1, 1941 at the age of 80.

The residue of the estate was left on terms which were not easy to administer, and on November 29, 1948 Mr. Justice Wynn-Parry approved a Scheme for the administration of the charity directed by her will. The terms of the testamentary gift were amended slightly by the Scheme, and the following extract shows in square brackets the words deleted from the will and underlines the words added by the Scheme:

the furtherance by lectures or otherwise among the Common People of [this country] <u>the United Kingdom of Great Britain and Northern Ireland</u> of the knowledge of the Comparative Jurisprudence and the Ethnology of the chief European Countries including [our own] <u>the United Kingdom</u> and the circumstances of the growth of such Jurisprudence to the intent that the Common People of [our Country] <u>the United Kingdom</u> may realise the privileges which in law and custom they enjoy in comparison with other European Peoples and realising and appreciating such privileges may recognise the responsibilities and obligations attaching to them.

These words now form the object of the charity as set out in clause 3 of the Scheme. The capitalisation follows that in Miss Hamlyn's will.

There are currently eight Trustees:

Professor J. A. Andrews, M.A., B.C.L., J.P.
Professor A. L. Diamond, LL.M. (Chairman)
The Rt. Hon. Lord Edmund-Davies
Professor D. S. Greer, B.C.L., LL.B.
Professor B. Hogan, LL.B.
Doctor Harry Kay, PH.D.
Professor A. I. Ogus, M.A., B.C.L.
Professor D. M. Walker, Q.C., M.A., PH.D., LL.D., F.B.A.

Immediately the Scheme for the Hamlyn trust was approved the Trustees initiated an annual series of lectures by outstanding individuals, and the published versions—"the book of the lectures"—are well known to lawyers and include several classics of scholarship on and concerning the law. They have received considerable notice in the press. The first series was given in 1949 by Mr. Justice Denning, and the full list appears on pp. vii and viii above. Lord Hailsham of St. Marylebone delivered the thirty-fifth Series of Hamlyn Lectures in May 1983 at Lincoln's Inn.

May 1983   AUBREY L. DIAMOND
                                    Chairman of the Trustees

The Theme

There have been thirty-four Hamlyn lecturers before me. I
am the thirty-fifth. It is time we asked ourselves where we are
going. Miss Hamlyn died in 1941. In November 1948 the
Chancery Division sanctified her generous bequest with only
modest changes in her language. But a will speaks from the
date of death, and in 1941 the war had four more weary years
to go. I was the junior subaltern, and, after th Colonel, the
Quartermaster and the Second in Command, the oldest
officer in a regular battalion of the Rifle Brigade. The Battle
of Britain was over. Hitler had called off his invasion, and was
turning towards the same disastrous course which had
destroyed Napoleon. Pearl Harbour, Stalingrad, Alamein,
the surrender of Italy, Normandy, the Rhine crossing and
ultimate victory were all in the future. The Beveridge Report
had not been published. The Butler Education Act had not
been introduced into the House of Commons.

Yet Miss Hamlyn wrote her bequest in a triumphalist
mood. Let my lecturers, she says, tell the Common People of
the United Kingdom what privileges they enjoy and responsibilities and burdens they undertake by the simple fact of

being British. Let them study the ethnology and institutions of
Europe (I am not quite sure what she meant by ethnology in
the context of the trust) and compare their institutions and
jurisprudence with our own, and they must see how lucky
they are to be British and what a serious responsibility is
therefore imposed on us who enjoy the privilege. As the years
rolled by, her lecturers have looked at their remit with growing scepticism. Miss Hamlyn's triumphalism was echoed by
the first lecturer, Mr. Justice Denning as he then was, a sort of
proto-Denning I might call him, who had not yet acquired the
distinctive style of his later years. But by 1974 Lord Scarman
found the founder's language "somewhat dated"—dated
because of the self-confidence which it expressed. It has also
been described as "quaint." In his lectures Professor Wade
even confessed to "an uneasy conscience" and could no more
than express the "hope," but without much confidence, that
he would "see Miss Hamlyn's shade" on the other side of the
Styx "waiting for me reproachfully." Other lecturers have
taken refuge in byways, sometimes of considerable sophistica-
tion. When I was first invited to enjoy the honour of being the
thirty-fifth lecturer I prudently acquired a selection of the
more recent lectures, in particular those of Lord Scarman, Sir
Norman Anderson, Lord MacKenzie Stuart, Professor
Wade, and last, but not least, the late Mr. Hubert Monroe,
whose racy, learned, and beautifully written exposition of,
and diatribe against, the income tax laws, though they would
have astonished the pious foundress, and bewildered her
"Common People," gave me as much pleasure as any of
them. Since then Professor Honoré has favoured me with his
more orthodox *The Quest for Security* in which he faces the
challenge of comparison with Europe, but reaches no very
clear conclusion on the supposed superiority of British

jurisprudence and institutions at least in the limited fields of his chosen subjects in human relationships.

All this has led me to believe that I must face the problem squarely. As, broadly speaking, I am in sympathy with Miss Hamlyn's point of view, I am not afraid of meeting her on the other side of the Styx. I wish to take her shade firmly by the hand and conduct her back on to the hither bank, so that she may examine for herself the new conditions in which her lecturer must operate. So much has changed since she spoke from death in 1941 that I am sure she would wish the case to be restated along the whole front for the "Common People" in 1983, and she will find, of course, that the context in which these lectures now have to be delivered is so different that many of the assumptions implicit in the original bequest must be enlarged, examined, revised, and turned over and over before we can ask the Common People to accept the lesson which Miss Hamlyn wished them to learn.

Nevertheless, my first words to the pious foundress must be of reassurance. She evidently believed that the "Common People" had only to be instructed in certain ascertainable facts to be able to see how much better off they are here than, and here I quote her words with an intention to qualify them later, the "other European Peoples," on condition, but only on condition, that they are also made aware (and here I quote again) of the responsibilities and obligations which they enjoy as the "Common People of the United Kingdom." She will find, of course, that the "Common People" of the United Kingdom is not by any means the same thing as those whom she wished to instruct in 1941. She will also find that the comparison with "the other European peoples" is no longer apt, for these are now in two widely separate groups, West and East, and the comparison is not the same. She will find too that, in making the comparison, the field of Europe is now itself far too narrow. We will have to talk about North and South, the Third World, and underdeveloped nations as well as of Europe, East and West. Our comparison must extend to the United States, Australia, Canada, New Zealand and South Africa. We shall have to pay visits to the Indian Sub-continent, the Middle East, South East Asia, Black Africa, South America, and even China, before the comparison can be made valid. Yet, at the end of the day, the foundress may be reassured. We are accustomed so much to discuss in more or less derogatory language our present woes, our economic and political shortcomings, our industrial strife, our arrogant and predatory trade unions, our alleged political polarisation, our one-purpose pressure groups, our violence, and triviality and vulgarity of our media, the deficiencies of our voting system, our processes of legislation, the supposed limitations of our judiciary, that it has become almost a paradox that a lecturer should seek to address "the Common People of the United Kingdom" in the bland belief that it is a "privilege" to be one of them. But Miss Hamlyn has nothing to fear from me, at least on this score. I believe we are still a happier country to live in than any other, or than almost any other, in the world and that those who might challenge successful comparison with ourselves are precisely those who resemble us most closely. It remains a privilege to enjoy British laws, traditions, customs, immunities and institutions. It remains an obligation to keep this so. So whilst Miss Hamlyn's shade has many surprises, and some shocks, in store for her, with the necessary adjustments and qualifications, her present lecturer is still prepared to stand by what she said in 1941.

First Shock:
The Common People

Miss Hamlyn's first shock will be to identify "the Common People of the United Kingdom" to whom she wished her lecturer to address himself. I will assume she knew already something about the two communities in Northern Ireland. But in 1941 I think it fair to suppose that she thought that the status quo was there to stay. That Stormont should be abolished, that Northern Ireland should be governed from Whitehall, and should lock up many major units of our armed forces in an endeavour to keep the peace, and murderers and torturers at bay, I do not believe she would have envisaged. I would have expected her to think that the status quo which had lasted from 1922 and was to endure until 1969, when the troubles began, would remain permanent, and that she would be as horrified as I am at what is going on there now, and as little inclined as I am to regard it as a privilege to be an inhabitant of the six remaining counties of the province of Ulster. But in making this admission, I think she would have said that this is what comes of not regarding sufficiently the second part of her thesis, the obligations of citizenship and the duties of good neighbourliness which the privilege imposes.

Whether she would have been right in that might be open to question, though not by me. I would happen to agree with her. But I do not intend to carry that discussion further.

Nevertheless, she may well be more than puzzled to identify the Common People of the mainland of Britain. What weight would she have expected her thirty-fifth lecturer to give to movements like Scottish nationalism, Plaid Cymru or the Welsh Language Society, to refer only to the ancient races, present for centuries in one part of the United Kingdom or another, the English, the Scots, the Welsh, and the Irish of two cultures whether in their homeland of Ulster, or present and voting in Birmingham, Liverpool, Glasgow, or Kilburn? But, as Sir Norman Anderson amongst others very clearly recognised, the difficulty does not rest with these. I shall have to introduce Miss Hamlyn to the so-called ethnic minorities, most, though not all, of whom have come to inhabit the United Kingdom in the forty odd years (a short enough time in any reckoning) which have elapsed since she designed her series of lectures. How would she counsel her lecturers to address the Cypriots (Greek or Turkish) in North London, or the Chinese from Hong Kong, Singapore or Malaysia who have made their homes here, and brought up families? What does Miss Hamlyn have to say in the wake, for instance, of the report of my predecessor as the Hamlyn lecturer, Lord Scarman, on the riots in Brixton, Toxteth and Moss Side? How would she ask her lecturer to address the shopkeepers of Hindu or Moslem origin who have set up shop in my own London village of Roehampton, or who tread the sodden streets of Bradford, Ealing or Birmingham, driven from their homelands, possibly by poverty, or the desire simply to improve their lot, or perhaps by the discriminatory racialist legislation in East Africa where their industry and highly organised home life had given them a place of sojourn some-times for three or four generations? Clearly, in speaking of the "Common People," the pious foundress postulated some common denominator, some basic homogeneity in the audience her lecturer was to address. But has not the former Master of the Rolls, the first of Miss Hamlyn's lecturers, in the original version of his latest book, claimed that there was no such homogeneity, and did he not suggest that this want of homogeneity was a matter of sufficient seriousness to warrant the abolition of random selection among jurors, surely one of the institutions a Hamlyn lecturer ought to defend? Coming from so eminent a source this is a claim to which at least consideration must be given though I myself cannot endorse his view. I do not believe that Miss Hamlyn would have wished her thirty-fifth lecturer to shirk this issue. When, however, she had got over her first shock at the new elements, European, Asian, and African, introduced into the popula-tion of the "Common People" in the years following the war—and I am sure it would have been a shock—I fancy Miss Hamlyn's shade might take a more robustly optimistic view than Lord Denning's of the British scene. I fancy she might find herself strongly reinforced in her belief in the value of and necessity for her lectures. Disregarding for a moment the mysterious reference to ethnology, which might cut either way, I believe she might well say that, if our institutions have an inherent value of their own as making a firm structure for a stable society, it was more than ever necessary to analyse and expound the essential nature of the structure, and to explain its virtues. I feel even more sure that she would have added that it was more than ever necessary to propound to the "Common People" her belief that the continued enjoyment of their privileges was conditional on the recognition of the responsibility owed by each to their preservation, and the acknowledgment of the responsibility to be borne by those who possessed them.

As to the lack of homogeneity, which formed such an obstacle to the former Master of the Rolls, and which at present forms a recurrent theme in the public speeches of some prominent politicians, I hope she would adopt a robustly questioning and sceptical attitude. What exactly is meant by "homogeneity"? Have we ever enjoyed it? If it means a common citizenship, together with the obligations of personal loyalty, dedication to the natural virtues of honesty, family solidarity, personal voluntary service of all kinds, willingness to forgo personal gain for public good, acceptance that in the end the nation must be defended against external aggression and internal disruption, in so far as it involves abstention from violence of all kinds in defiance of law, one must accept that this is the price we pay for living in a stable and respectable society with common norms of behaviour, mutual respect, and a capacity for self-government. Miss Hamlyn would have no difficulty in her lecturer preaching this. A free society cannot be forever disputing about fundamentals, pursuing individual or sectional interests, or talking as if there were no limit to the extent to which a majority—often more properly a highly organised minority—can dominate minority groups, or it will simply cease to be free, even if for a time it maintains the outward semblance of free institutions developed in a happier age. A free society needs cement as well as liberty to differ. It requires such virtues as self-discipline consciously imposed, respect for established authority openly preached and advocated.

But, if homogeneity means uniformity, as I fear Lord Denning may have unconsciously assumed, then I would suggest that, in a complicated modern state, it is neither possible nor desirable. I believe that Miss Hamlyn would take heart, amongst other things, from the history of Anglo Jewry during her own lifetime, and after it. There was a vast influx of Eastern European Jews into our various cities onwards from the later nineteenth century. These were refugees from the pogrom and other forms of discrimination in Czarist Russia. So late as the 1930s, when I first practised in Whitechapel County Court, there was a permanent Yiddish interpreter attached to the court, and later, when the advance of Hitler presaged the ultimate holocaust, the numbers of immigrants from that source were constantly being increased. When I was a boy, anti-semitism was even intellectually respectable, and often unconsciously assumed, as much by so-called Liberals as by others. Both Belloc and Chesterton were distinctly anti-semitic in tone, as, at the other end of the political spectrum, were Kipling and, I think, Saki. Yet, as time has gone on, Anglo Jewry, without being absorbed into something non-Jewish, has become a valued, loyal, and respectable part of the British establishment, enriching cultural, economic and political life, and that without positive discrimination in its favour. I see no reason why, in due course, if it is allowed to operate naturally and without self-assertion, or attempts to cut corners, the same cannot be true of the industrious and adaptable Indian, Chinese, Cypriot and African minorities in our midst. On the whole this has happened, more or less successfully, in the United States, and in this country the problem is surely less severe, because it is unaccompanied by the difficulties associated with the servile origin which have beset some at least of the minorities in North America.

There is at least one common denominator for all of us who can claim to be part of the Common People of the United Kingdom, and I say this without disrespect to the Welsh Language Society, the Gaelic enthusiasts and other minority languages. It is the English tongue, and the system of freedom

under law with which it will be forever associated, and which
was the subject chosen by Miss Hamlyn's first lecturer, Mr.
Justice Denning. It was not a modern English writer, who, in
the face of multilingualism in this very island, but in an earlier
age, penned the immortal words:

> "Lerid and Lewid, old and young
> All understanden English tongue."

This is no place to pursue this aspect of the subject. Miss
Hamlyn's trust was not concerned with linguistics. But we
have more than English in common, and as I consider the
various ways in which our institutions have developed in the
past 35 years, I shall seek to spell out, not uncritically but
firmly, the abiding value of our evolving institutioins, changing constantly, but still I trust true to their original dynamic. In
the result I seek to make an audience to myself, by trying to
face the increasingly diverse elements in our population with
the necessity to address our common problems by insisting on
our common interest in a stable, secure and peaceful society.
For such a society must be based on a firm tradition, secure
institutions, and abiding standards of value. It must be con-
trolled by law and command general respect. It must be
inspired by our traditional love of freedom, and the belief in
traditional values to which we still cling, despite increasing
chaos and tyranny in the world. It must stand firm against the
threats of modern military technology, the bombs which deal
death indiscriminately, the murder weapons of sub-machine
guns, and the instruments of mass destruction of which the
nuclear range is only one and not necessarily the most lethal.
My appeal to the Common People is based on my belief in the
infinite value of the individual human soul, the sanctity of the

human family, and the natural propensity we all have to love our fellow man, described long ago by Cicero as the foundation of all law (*fundamentum juris*). My appeal to the Common People is based on common needs, common dangers, and common hopes, and it must be directed towards a common purpose.

Second Shock:
The International Dimension

I fear that Miss Hamlyn's shade is now in for a second shock. Not only the Common People has changed its identity. When she wrote her will, she made a further series of assumptions, based on the continuance of a status quo in international law which has since radically changed. The world of international law is based upon a congeries of sovereign national states. In 1941 and despite the Versailles and Lausanne treaties the institutions which Miss Hamlyn was instructing her lecturers to compare favourably with others were basically the consequences of the status quo ante 1914 and not just of 1939. They were partly the cause and partly the effect of an unbroken series of successes which had resulted in a hundred years of comparative peace in Europe, and a British hegemony in the international field. As a result, about a quarter of the world's surface and about a quarter of the world's population were ruled more or less directly from Whitehall. In addition the independent nations of the Commonwealth, including at that time South Africa, had derived their institutions largely from those evolved here during the nineteenth century. The Partridge cartoons in *Punch* still depicted a proud lion sur-

13

ounded by half-grown cubs. We can now see of course that
he Great War of 1914 had in fact largely undermined the
whole basis of this status quo. But, even at the end of the last
war, the façade replaced by the victorious alliance still remained surprisingly unaltered, and, owing to the steadfast
and heroic resistance to Hitler, while Miss Hamlyn was leaving her will in 1941, British prestige had hardly ever stood so
high.

We can now see that the international climate in which Miss
Hamlyn's thirty-fifth lecture has to be delivered is altogether
different, though how far it is better is more easily open to
question. Speaking for myself, I utterly refuse to condemn
colonialism, or to regard its liquidation during the period
under review as an unmixed blessing. Most countries which
came under British rule were governed on the whole better
than they had ever been governed before, or have ever been
governed since. It would be naive to claim that the whole
thing was disinterested. But under what system of government have the rulers ever been wholly disinterested? The
ideal of the Imperialists of the Milner's kindergarten type was
no contemptible thing. As one can read from the literature of
the time, that ideal consisted in a belief in a growing circle of
developing nations, each evolving steadily towards self-
government under the tutelage of the Crown, living at peace
internally and with one another, joined in a sort of loose
confederation, with freedom of trade, freedom of movement,
incorrupt courts, strong and compatible legal systems, a per-
vasive and growing use of the English language, and practising
a sort of non-denominational Christianity. There was nothing
ignoble or foolish about this ideal, either in comparison with
what had gone before it, or with what has actually followed its
dissolution. Those who deride Kipling and his ideals had
better make fresh comparisons with the present. The Milner

kindergarten was neither a conspiracy of bad men, nor an assembly of fools. With hindsight, of course, one may see that, with other things, the calamity of the First World War destroyed it as a feasible possibility, and that it was brought to an end abruptly by the events which followed the Second World War; in particular by the Cold War, by the hostility of the American republic to its continuance, by the great drive against colonialism in the Third World, and by the internal weakness produced by the opposition to its continuance by left wing politicians. In the result, its collapse was inevitable. But what has followed it in practice has not destroyed its claim to good repute.

It remains true that Miss Hamlyn was unaware of its impending demise when she made her will. On the contrary, I believe that like the rest of us she believed in its survival. She certainly could not have realised the impact which its destruction would inevitably have upon those institutions which she wished her lecturers to applaud. After the enfranchisement of its parts, the Indian Empire was first divided and then subdivided, and its severed parts have since been engaged in at least three major wars with one another. The territories mandated to Britain and France, through the whole of which, from Cairo to the Turkish border, from Beirut to the Persian Gulf, I was able in 1941 to pass in perfect safety by staff car, by train or on foot, have been divided and shaken by war and terrorism, and these not only between Israel and her Arab neighbours. Lebanon has been shattered. Iraq has been engaged in bitter warfare with Shi'ite Iran. South and North Yemen have fought, and the uneasy truce between Greece and Turkey has been broken at least twice by the partition of Cyprus. Whether one looks at South East Asia, where the dissolution of the French Empire has been followed by a series of unspeakable horrors, or at Africa, where Uganda,

Libya, Egypt, Ghana and Nigeria have been the scene of constant civil war or revolution, or at Southern Africa, the collapse of the *Pax Britannica* has been disastrous in its immediate consequence to the very people who were demanding an end to colonialism and expected to benefit most from its demise. Emphatically it must now be established beyond question that, though the demise of colonial rule may have given rise to doubts about the efficacy of our traditional institutions, it most certainly has not increased the general security or happiness of mankind. Of the various institutions which the Milner kindergarten sought to transplant to alien soil, Sandhurst appears alone to have flourished, while the Temple and Westminster seem largely to have withered and died.

But it is with Europe and Britain that Miss Hamlyn was primarily concerned. Yet here, too, the whole structure has altered. No one on this side of its great divide desired the partition of Europe into two hostile camps, and no one in the immediate aftermath of victory expected it. All hopes were centred on the new United Nations Organisation situated in a newly interventionist United States which now for the first time abandoned its former isolationist posture. How we all hoped that the allies in war might continue in friendship after the restoration of peace, would restore unity to a shattered and desperate world, and freedom and life to the peoples of the former Fascist allies. Instead Marxism-Leninism has emerged as the dominant ideology of the vast Communist empires of the Soviet Union and China, whose alienation from the West and from one another has rendered impotent the very institution which it had been hoped would provide a firm structure for peace and security in a war weary world.

It is not a future which Miss Hamlyn foresaw in 1941, nor one of which she would have approved. What, however, these revolutionary changes have not achieved is to disprove her general thesis of the superiority of our own internal institutions over others, or the efficacy and efficiency of our ideal of responsible freedom under the rule of law over all rival systems when such a series of institutions can be established and made secure by the sense of responsibility and service which she sought to engender among those who enjoyed them.

At least there is no difficulty in discharging one duty of a Hamlyn lecturer in terms which the pious foundress would heartily applaud. Seventy years have elapsed since the Russian Revolution, and, in that time, if it was ever capable of success, Marxism-Leninism has had ample time to succeed, and it has proved a dismal failure, economically, philosophically, politically and morally. Its repeated bad harvests in what should potentially have proved one of the most fertile agricultural regions of the world, requiring constant importations of basic foods from freer countries, can no longer be ascribed to the vagaries of nature. Its total inability to produce consumer goods on a scale to satisfy its peoples can no longer be excused as due to the inadequate industrial base from which it started. Its inability after nearly three quarters of a century to achieve the withering away of the state into the Utopia of Communism can no longer be explained away by the malevolence of a vanished Imperialism, or the shortage of time necessary to achieve its end. The only thing it has ever proved good at is the use of force, and the only hope for the future of its peoples are the very internal stresses and strains which it describes as contradictions when found in the liberal democracies and which in them it partly engenders and partly attempts to exploit. But such stresses and strains are endemic in the human condition and occur in Marxist societies no less than those of the West.

This dismal scene, however, is not the only change to which Miss Hamlyn's shade will require to adjust itself. When I said a moment ago that, as the result of the Second World War, the structure of Europe had been transformed, I was not thinking only, and perhaps not mainly, of the Iron Curtain. I was thinking of the European Community, and the Council of Europe with its Convention on Human Rights. In returning to her field of reference, Miss Hamlyn's shade will have to take account of these. Shorn of her Imperial splendours, slowly and in part reluctantly, Britain and her institutions have had to come to terms with each of these, and two at least of Miss Hamlyn's lecturers, Lord Scarman and Lord MacKenzie Stuart, have made them a particular subject of scrutiny. I do not propose to cover their ground again. Like Miss Hamlyn, I am preoccupied with changes in our own institutions, and I am therefore concerned with the extent to which these have been altered by our obligations to these new associations. Nevertheless, the need to preserve our national identity within the new European structures is a problem which her lecturer cannot fail to confront in his panegyric of our domestic institutions.

The point to which this is leading up is that the efficiency and value of our internal relations must be measured in terms of our changed international position, and relative strength. Increasingly during the eighteenth century and the period of Antonine peace between 1815 and 1914, these were protected and left self-standing by the unassailable position enjoyed by the British Islands, the world-wide empire, the two-power navy, the gold standard, the industrial superiority which we had achieved by our lead in technology, and the immense commercial strength centred on the City of London. The inter-war period may be regarded as years of transition in which we were still looking backwards, hoping for reversion to a normality which never returned. Moral and social values may be enduring. But throughout the period of the Hamlyn lectures our institutions have been continuously constrained to adapt themselves to the change in our situation. Neither our industry, our currency, our defence, nor, ultimately, our political or legal institutions are protected or self-standing, and the failure of the United Nations to achieve a secure base of ordered international society has compelled us more and more to have recourse to alliances and international organisations. These range from NATO to the European Community, from internationally based companies to relationships with oil-producing countries in the Middle East. The total effect has been to restrict our freedom of action, and to compel us to harmonise and coordinate both our institutions and our legal systems with those with whom we cooperate. In the background the great divide between East and West has accentuated and accelerated the process which I have endeavoured to describe. To use the language of *1066 and All That*, we are no longer top nation (whatever this half humorous phrase may have meant), and with this fact Miss Hamlyn's lecturer must come to terms if he is to carry out faithfully Miss Hamlyn's prescription.

I have a fairly clear picture in my mind of the late Miss Hamlyn, and what she stood for. I think my picture of her is likely to be accurate as I have had many constituents in my time whose views were very much in the mould of Miss Hamlyn's mind. She was, I would fancy, both more robust and more conservative (with a small "c") than I. She would have been less haunted than I at the prospect of a third world war. She would have been more reluctant than I to see Britain a member of the Community. I suspect she would have been openly contemptuous of the Strasbourg Court of Human Rights. But she would have shared my disappointment at the performance of the United Nations. In her hostility to the Soviet Union she would have been more robust than I, and much more sympathetic to the response by Republican administrations in the United States.

I must pursue these issues with her since they all affect the matters with which these lectures are concerned. I do not apologise for this, any more than I have apologised for my search for the Common People in my description of the first shock which Miss Hamlyn's shade would have received on her return from across the Styx. Her lecturers have concentrated too closely, I believe, on the purely legal aspects of the instructions in Miss Hamlyn's will, and have underestimated the extent to which these in turn have been influenced by demographic (I suspect that this was what was meant by "ethnological" in the bequest) and social changes at home, and the international changes with which I have been concerned in my present study.

As I have said, I am haunted by the spectre of a third world war, which I believe would almost certainly become, if it did not begin as, a nuclear encounter. But I must, I think, begin with two criticisms of the so-called peace movement, which stem from an insufficient appreciation of the causes of war. The error began between the wars in the atmosphere of the Fulham by-election and the so-called peace ballot. Quite rightly, the "peace" enthusiasts believed that the origins of the First World War lay in the destabilisation of the relationship in relative power which began with a quite deliberate decision of policy by the German Imperial Government to challenge the supremacy of the Royal Navy at sea, a military fact which, more than anything else, lay at the root of the century of Antonine peace between 1815 and 1914. In the event, the peace movement of the inter-war years did more to bring about the Second World War than prevent it. Its members were quite wrong to attribute the outbreak of the Great War to the so-called arms race, as if the moral responsibility was equal. Quite simply, the arms race then and now is the consequence and not the cause of political tension. It is political tension or political ambition which creates an arms race and not vice versa, and, in so far as an established status quo of stability is destabilised, the immediate causes of the outbreak of war, even when largely unintended, are the result of that destabilisation. One of the symptoms prefiguring hostilities is the development of armed camps, the Triple Entente and the Triple Alliance in the period leading up to 1914, the German, Italian, and Japanese axis before 1939, and NATO and the Warsaw Pact at the present day. But these again are symptoms and not causes. It is quite impossible to attempt to treat the morality of the two sides as something about which an Olympian impartiality is acceptable, or to believe that the way to remove the causes of war is to ascribe blame to the symptoms. There was something inherently aggressive about the Kaiser's challenge, as there was about Hitler's Germany and as there was about Khrushchev's "we will bury you," and as there is in the present progressive increase in Soviet armaments. Relations between the fire and the fire brigade are not a proper field for judicial impartiality.

But morality or no, I continue to be haunted by the prospects of war resulting from present international anarchy. My reasons are two-fold. Quite simply, mankind desires peace, but almost invariably achieves war. With my old friend Lionel Curtis, I believe that the ultimate cause of war is the division of the human race into separate sovereignties. Unlike him, I regard the human race as much too various at the present time to be capable of any other type of organisation. We need time and the evolution of institutions before the promised time when wars shall be no more. At the end of the last war we had hoped that the United Nations would prove an effective instrument. Its failure is at once dangerous and disappointing. It was hoped to be the instrument by which sufficient powers of force would be in the grasp of those striving for peace to prevent a further outbreak of international bloodshed. Quite simply, the very forces which are the cause of war, the existence of sovereignty and rivalry at the top level, preserved realistically in the Charter in the power of veto, have completely destroyed its usefulness for this purpose.

The second cause of my anxiety is an observation of great perception made, so I had previously thought, by the Greek historian Thucydides, although I am not now sure of its authorship: "War is not fought about insignificant issues. It does arise out of insignificant incidents."

The great war between Athens and Sparta in the fifth century B.C. arose out of a riot and revolution in a colony of Corfu, into which the great powers were drawn because one party was allied with Corfu and consequentially Athens, and the other with Sparta's ally and Athens' rival, Corinth. The great war between Rome and Carthage began with a somewhat similar incident in an insignificant town in Spain, then on the edge of the civilised world. The great war which ended at Waterloo began with the capture of the Bastille, at that time containing, I believe, no more than seven political prisoners. An assassination of a relatively minor Royalty at Sarajevo led to the battles of Tannenberg and Passchendaele, the Russian Revolution, and the dissolution of the Turkish Empire in the Middle East. We all saw how relatively minor events in relatively remote places led to the cataclysm of 1939. War is not fought about insignificant issues. But it does arise out of apparently trivial incidents.

So I would say to Miss Hamlyn, whose general cast of mind

was surely more sanguine than my own, that if the pressure of events can lead to more juristically enforceable relationships between states, such as those involved in the Common Market and the European Convention, this may be no bad thing for humanity and for ourselves, and if we can avoid the major confrontation that I fear for long enough to enable such limitations on sovereignty (though initially she may disapprove) to have their full effect, this may well be a step in the right direction, and even in the shorter run may afford this country after the dissolution of its empire a greater measure of stability and protection for our institutions than we could otherwise obtain. To be preserved, our legal arrangements must take account of Community law, the European convention, and numerous other charters and conventions to which we are signatories.

Third Shock:
Elective Dictatorship

At first sight Miss Hamlyn's shade will be agreeably surprised at the sight of our main constitutional institutions. The traditional structures, Sovereign, Lords and Commons are still in place. Although criticisms of individual members of her family are perhaps a little more articulate and perhaps less acceptable in content than before, the Monarch is personally as popular as any of her Royal forbears, and the institution of Monarchy itself seems as well rooted as ever in the affections of the people. In spite of recurrent clamours for their abolition and reform, moderate changes in their powers and more or less radical changes in their composition, the Lords are, I believe, more popular and more efficient than in 1941. No effect has been given to the fundamental reforms proposed by dangerous radicals like Lord Hailsham, either in the direction of an elected second Chamber, devolved provincial government, or even the adoption into municipal law of the European Convention on Human Rights. Despite noises off by the SDP-Liberal alliance, both of the main political parties remain, to Professor Wade's dismay, strongly entrenched against any fundamental changes in our system of voting, at

25

any rate for the House of Commons. Indeed, at first sight and in this field the thirty-fifth Hamlyn lecturer will find it as easy to follow Miss Hamlyn's instructions as did the first.

On several points, she may immediately be reassured. I have no possible doubt that the separation of the headship of state from the leading political position in the government is an inestimable advantage, whether we accept Miss Hamlyn's prescription and compare our own hereditary sovereign with the presidents of the Fifth Republic in France, or cross the Atlantic and compare our own institutional head of state with either the comparatively reputable presidents of the United States or the comparatively disreputable presidents in Southern America. Still less have we anything to fear from the comparison if we travel further afield and compare the Cabinet system under a Prime Minister with the colourful, vain, and unstable presidents who strut and fret for a brief hour across the stage of the Third World. The difference is not merely that of separating the object of loyalty and national unity in the person of the Head of State from the subject of party political controversy in the person of the Head of Government. It is also that even on the purely governmental level the Cabinet system is intrinsically better, more flexible and more efficient than the presidential.

There are good reasons for this. The leaders of Government under a properly functioning Cabinet system are, in the nature of things, already experienced administrators, and seasoned men and women of affairs, well versed in national and international politics, and, in their colleagues, they possess experienced potential critics should they make mistakes, and valuable potential successors should they fall ill, become incapacitated or die. By contrast, under the presidential system, the executive is composed entirely of the president's own creatures, without a secure seat in the legislature, who disappear into the obscurity of business or academic life the moment their precarious tenures are at an end. Worse still, should a president die, or be assassinated, there usually lurks a second rate figure automatically entitled to succeed, and chosen for almost any reason except his suitability to do so.

Though my dislike of the only alternative model of republican constitution is less pronounced, I confess at once that the drab heads of state employed to carry out ceremonial duties as part of a republican state combining a Cabinet system with a ceremonial head of state present a far less attractive picture than our present hereditary monarchy, consisting as it does of a colourful personality sharing her functions with a whole spectrum of human beings of both sexes and all ages constantly providing occasions for secular festivals concerned with the whole drama of human life from birth to marriage, from health to sickness, from maturity to old age, and finally to the end which awaits us all. No one, I suppose, in the reign of Elizabeth I, or even her Hanoverian successors, would quite have imagined the popular but apolitical role played by her present Majesty Queen Elizabeth II. But then, strange as the obvious must constantly appear, the gift of prevision is denied to mortal man.

It is when one comes to contemplate the working parts of our constitution that I fancy that Miss Hamlyn is in for a bit of a shock, and her lecturer will have to answer certain questions, which, if he is to be honest, will cast some doubts as to the soundness of Miss Hamlyn's confident preference for the status quo.

Although, on the surface, our institutions are the same as they were at the turn of the century, by the time Miss Hamlyn died they were already changing, both in character and scale, and, in the 40 years following her death, they have gone on changing beyond recognition. Differences of scale become differences of kind, and the sheer size of government has made Parliament, the Ministry, the civil service, and, for that matter, almost every aspect of local government, wholly different in kind from the institutions which we are bidden to commend to the Common People. When Gladstone introduced his Home Rule Bill into Parliament in the 1880s, the first and second readings were debated in a leisurely fashion over 16 nights during a period of two months. The radical Lloyd George Budget of 1909 visualised central government expenditure of about £120 million (of course then in gold sovereigns). According to my recollection the whole annual budget of the inter-war periods ran at between £800 and £900 millions in the currency of that date. The reforming Liberal Government of 1911 enacted about 450 pages of public general legislation, and there was relatively little subordinate legislation. Today public expenditure is running, in contemporary currency, at about £130,000 million, of which about the largest single item represents interest on the national debt. Even the most important constitutional bills take, on second reading, about two days only and are nearly always guillotined and sent to small committees upstairs working to a timetable. The Labour Government of 1975 and the Conservative Government of 1979–80 each passed over 3,000 pages of public general legislation, with, I suppose, about 10,000 additional pages of secondary legislation into the bargain. With all these powers, practically no recent government has had a majority of the electorate behind it. Yet almost every government has claimed an almost indefeasible right or "mandate" to enact every item of its manifesto into law, almost without regard to possible criticisms of it in debate and sometimes without regard to practical difficulties encountered after the assumption of office. None of these features can be scrutinised without some disquiet by any lover of parliamentary institutions.

Quite apart from the activities of central and local government, the various nationalisation statutes, and the activities of various statutory and non-statutory quangos, the rise of local nationalisms, Scots and Welsh, the continued constitutional deadlock in Northern Ireland, and the total failure of successive governments to base local taxation on anything more satisfactory than rates plus a rate support grant, clearly raise questions unknown in 1941 about our basic constitutional arrangements. Are we right to stick to a unitary state instead of making terms, if not to federalism, at least to some form of devolved provincial government? Though the House of Lords is certainly a more efficient and vigorous debating chamber than in the days of Gilbert and Sullivan, is not the principle of nomination, upon which all except hereditary peerages are based, if anything more objectionable than inherited right? Is not the House of Commons too large and its sphere of responsibilities too multifarious to enable it to discharge its work efficiently? Are the two major parties wise to stick to our traditional system of first past the post voting? Is not the field of delegated legislation and ministerial power so wide, and is not the examination of even primary legislation so cursory, as to suggest that some internal means of questioning it by reference to a general statement of human rights is desirable? Different answers may be given to these questions. But the questions arise and, in my opinion, will not go away. In my time I have attempted answers to most of them, and to most of them my proposed answers have either been ignored or treated as unacceptable. Perhaps I would be unwise to repeat any of them now. My opinion, for what it is worth, is that, if they or any of them are ever accepted, they will be accepted piecemeal, and then only as the result of crisis. But, in the meantime, I simply express my unabated faith in the validity of our essential structure. In spite of the changes, our system has nothing to fear from comparison with others. For all its defects our Cabinet system of government is superior to any other, and in particular to the presidential. It produces better informed, more experienced, and more moderate political leaders. Our unwritten constitution is more flexible and sophisticated than any of your written constitutions shackled by rigid amending formulae. Whatever the defects of the present House of Lords, and whatever the desirability (as I think) of replacing it with an elected second Chamber without life peerages, bishops, or hereditary legislators, it is a useful body as it stands, and does much to mitigate the shortcomings of the House of Commons. Whatever the arguments for proportional representation and its numerous variants, our two main parties are right to suspect, as undermining the stability of executive government and of democracy itself, any changes likely to produce a multiplicity of parties. Our adherence to the European Convention and the Strasbourg Court may not be a substitute for introducing the European Convention as a direct influence on our national courts. None the less we can still claim to live under a system inherently more agreeable than any other that I can personally think of. Miss Hamlyn continues to be justified in asking her lecturers to expound its virtues. That is, she is justified on one condition, which she herself prescribed.

The condition is that people recognise that the possession of such a system is a privilege and that those who wish to continue to live under it must themselves accept a personal responsibility for its preservation. After his defeat in the presidential general election, I seem to remember that Mr. Jimmy Carter was asked what in his opinion was the greatest enemy of individual liberty, and I seem to remember that he replied: "the single purpose pressure group." If my memory is correct, I think he had a point. Indeed I think he had two points, and these both valuable. In the first place, he never suggested that such groups should be made illegal (unless of course their objects amount to a criminal conspiracy, and he was not talking about these). The point he made is moral, not legal. It is based on the moral responsibility of every group and individual not to pursue even lawful objectives too far. In the second place, the defeated ex-president did not seek to differentiate between pressure groups with desirable and those with undesirable objects. Within the law, in a free society, what is desirable or not as a matter for association must be a matter of free choice, and the criteria for deciding this question must be subjective. When Aneurin Bevan said that priorities were the religion of socialism he was understating a good case. All responsible governments, socialist or otherwise, are compelled to formulate policies at any one time by making hard choices between different courses of otherwise desirable action rendered incompatible with one another by limitations of available means or available time. For this purpose it does not really matter very much whether a pressure group is a trade union, a society for the protection of the environment, for the promotion of divorce reform, the elimination of racial discrimination, the reduction of taxation or the increase of retirement pensions for the elderly. It may be that some or all of these objectives are opposed on principle. But those who support them and wish to press them upon governments have really more than one question to ask themselves before they adopt any particular course of action. The first, no doubt, is the inherent desirability of their objective. But, unless they wish to become the enemies of a free and ordered society, they must, after they have answered the first question in their favour, ask themselves at least two further questions before they embark upon a particular course. The first is whether the means proposed in the particular case are legitimate. The second is whether the particular end they have in view can be justified in comparison with the other legitimate needs, aims, or aspirations of other members of society who may not join with them in their particular objectives. It may be a desirable object to "Ban the Bomb," and at the same time wrong to disfigure a beautiful building with the words. It may be legitimate to seek more pay and at the same time wrong to penalise the sick or those with other legitimate needs in order to achieve it. It may be right to seek a reduction in taxation, but wrong in a particular international situation at the expense of defence. In the end, Miss Hamlyn is justified again. In comparison with those of others, our institutions do survive well, but only on condition that their possession is treated as a privilege and as imposing a heavy responsibility for their preservation on all who live under them. We enjoy a representative system of government based on universal adult franchise. It will endure so long, and only so long, as our fellow countrymen use their powers within the limitations required for its survival.

Fourth Shock:
Due Process of Law

Among the most important of the institutions with which Miss Hamlyn would expect her lecturers to deal are those connected with the rule and due process of law. The expression "due process" is heard nowadays more often on American than on English lips. But its origin is rooted firmly in English law. So far as I know, it occurs first in Norman French in the Statute 28 Edward III c.3 (1354). In its present English form it occurs in the Petition of Right of 1627 and the Habeas Corpus Act 1640 (to trace its history no further). I am not qualified to follow Miss Hamlyn's prescription that I should compare our own due process with that of Continental countries which, to a greater or lesser degree, follow the Code Napoléon. There are, however, certain criteria for due process under any system. These must include an independent judiciary, a fair hearing in accordance with the rules of natural justice, total absence of oppression whether judicial, political or popular, access to the courts, public hearings and the availability, at least in serious cases, of advice and representation by an independent and incorrupt legal profession. Efficiency and dispatch are also qualities with which no process of law can afford to dispense.

It is worthwhile pointing to certain differences between our own and Continental systems. To the end of his days, my father fondly but mistakenly believed that in Continental systems there was no presumption of innocence. This is not so (*cf.* European Convention on Human Rights, Article 6, paragraph 2). But what is true is that, in common law systems, the function of the court is quite different from that prevailing on the Continent. On the Continent, the function of the court is inquisitorial. It is there to discover the truth. A group of distinguished Italian jurists who came to consult me as to the reason for the greater expedition with which criminal cases are disposed of here (I found this enquiry somewhat encouraging) were astonished, disconcerted, and, I thought, a little shocked when I had to explain at the outset that this function was not the function of an English court. Its function is to decide whether, and to what extent, the prosecution, or in civil cases the plaintiff, has proved its case. This difference runs right through the whole judicial process. A Continental advocate does not ordinarily examine or cross-examine witnesses. If witnesses are examined orally, I understand the court plays the principal role. It would be fruitless for my present purpose to pursue the matter further.

A second difference is the fact that, under most Continental systems, judges form a separate profession. Like British judges they have security of tenure. But they are not, and have never been, practising lawyers. They form part of the civil service. They leave law school at the age, say, of about 27, and they then become judges. Many years later, if they do well, they reach the top of the judicial service. In all common law countries, judges are appointed from more or less successful members of the practising profession, in England barristers or solicitors. In America such judges are elected directly or appointed by the executive. Both American systems have manifest disadvantages from the point of view of judicial independence and impartiality. In England an honourable, but comparatively recent, tradition insulates judicial appointments, as well as judicial security of tenure, from political pressures. My own view is that this is one of the main tests of a good Lord Chancellor.

I mention only one more difference of importance, the lay magistracy, which is virtually unique to England and Wales, though in Switzerland an even more spectacular system exists, under which laymen man even the equivalent of the High Court Bench. Outside Switzerland Continental lawyers are astonished, and even a little aghast, when I tell them that about 98 per cent. of our criminal trials take place before judges without legal qualifications, and to the very general public satisfaction. As Lord Chancellor I can testify to the fact that by far the bitterest and most frequent complaints I receive from the public relate to the professional judiciary. Again, as Lord Chancellor, I can claim that appointments are not political. Although active members of all parties sit on the magisterial bench, no recent Lord Chancellor has shown political bias, and there exists an elaborate system which effectively prevents him from doing so.

With all this, Miss Hamlyn's shade would be tolerably familiar. But it would be prudent at this stage that I should begin to prepare her for a further series of shocks. The first will relate to the jury system. The second will deal with administrative law. The third consists in the proliferation of tribunals outside the range of the ordinary courts. The fourth consists in the provision of legal aid, civil and criminal. Fifth, and perhaps most important of all, I must discuss the, to my mind growing, threat to the independence of the judiciary, and to the prestige and authority of the judicial office.

English law has not progressed at a regular speed throughout its history. It has had its creative periods, and its periods of quiescence and consolidation. In part, its creativity has been due to bold strokes of imagination by creative and original judges, like Lord Mansfield, Lord Blackburn, Lord Atkin, or, in our own time, amongst others by Lords Reid and Denning. In part it has been due to external forces like the original thinking of Jeremy Bentham or the social and political activity of Parliament. The two sources are complementary and interacting, and in more recent years have been rendered more fruitful and effective by the labours of such bodies as the two Law Commissions, the Law Reform Committee and the Criminal Law Revision Committee.

My father's professional and political life was spent very largely in a period of consolidation. If I were asked to put a term to it I would begin at 1900 and continue it until and including the decisions in *Liversidge* v. *Anderson* and *Duncan* v. *Cammell Laird*. During that period, and despite the occasional landmark decision like *Donoghue* v. *Stevenson* and some remarkable individual judgments, it almost looked as if the common law had run out of steam. Contrast this, for instance, with the creativity shown by Lord Reid alone in the single twelve-month period covered by [1964] *Appeal Cases*. I would mark my new period as beginning in 1946 with the decision of Denning J. (as he then was) in the *High Trees* case and as continuing until the present day. In part, of course, the period of creativity has been brought about by the pressure upon the judiciary of constantly changing social circumstances, and the totally different relationship between authority and the individual, and between the individual and various types of independent corporations or associations like trade unions. In part it has been brought about by the vastly increasing body of legislation, primary and secondary, and the need in every case to interpret it and apply it to individual cases.

But, whatever the causes, English law is a totally different thing from what it was when I was called to the Bar in 1932 and what, no doubt, in 1941 Miss Hamlyn still considered it to be. Dicey had taken great pride in the fact that in English law there was no such thing as *Droit Administratif*. Already by 1970, the fourth edition of Halsbury begins with the hitherto novel title *Administrative Law*. The remedies against authority, now rendered infinitely more easy of access and far more widely available by the process of judicial review embodied in Order 53 of the Rules of the Supreme Court and the various judicial decisions under both the old and the new procedures, the devices of the *Mareva* injunction and the *Anton Piller* order, the various developments in the law of arbitration, the growing limitations on the doctrine of sovereign immunity developing in parallel with the commercial activities of state trading organisations, all mark a period of almost unprecedented creativity.

In my enthusiasm I find that I have strayed far too far from my original plan of proclaiming English law to the Common People. I must retrace my steps. There is practically no single institution which has shaped English law, civil or criminal, more decisively than the jury. When my father was called to the Bar almost every issue of fact that came before the superior courts outside the Chancery Division was tried by a jury. Even in the county courts cases were tried by juries (I think of seven). Incidentally these still linger on in theory, and when I last enquired six cases in a single year were so tried, though I have no idea where they were heard, or what they were about. Every court in the King's Bench Division was designed with a jury box, almost invariably filled, either with a common jury, a special jury, or, in rarer commercial cases, a special jury of the City of London. In default of defence in a High Court case, unliquidated damages were assessed by a sheriff's jury summoned to Red Lion Square. There was provision for compensation to be fixed by a jury in cases of compulsory acquisition. Coroners almost always sat with a jury. Grand juries (usually consisting of county magistrates) acted as an additional sieve to committal by justices before trial by indictment. Juries of matrons were empanelled to discover whether a woman on trial for her life was pregnant. Juries determined whether a prisoner who would not plead was mute of malice or by the visitation of God. Readers of Surtees will remember how the unfortunate Jorrocks became, by the verdict of a jury, a lunatic so found. All this was in addition to the ordinary petty juries sitting on indictments in the Courts of Quarter Sessions and Assizes, or at the Old Bailey.

Most of this elaborate system was still intact when the Great War broke out in 1914. Much of it still remains intact in the United States, that great museum of discarded English legal forms, in the Republic of Ireland, and, apart from the Diplock courts, in Northern Ireland as well where they cling to their old mumpsimus with all the fanaticism of the illiterate priest in the story. But in England, apart from a few cases of fraud or defamation, the civil jury is almost a thing of the past, and the great race of civil jury advocates which sustained the reputation of the English Bar from Erskine to Walter Monckton is extinct as the dodo.

I do not myself regret its passing. Its weaknesses as an instrument of civil justice are known to everyone who has operated it. There is the danger of disagreement, involving a fresh trial, sometimes more than one, with, for the litigants,

renewed anxiety and costs thrown away. There is the com-
promise verdict which necessarily involves injustice to both
sides. All civil trials by jury tend, if fought to the end, to last a
third longer (at least) than trials before judge alone. We have
all known examples of the perverse verdict against the weight
of the evidence. There is the tendency of juries to find for an
injured plaintiff and for excessive sums. There is the additional hazard of good, and bad, professional advocacy unduly
influencing the result. In addition there are, or rather there
were, the absurdly artificial rules of evidence by which the
profession sought to hedge about these weaknesses.

Will the jury survive indefinitely as the only method of trial
in criminal cases on indictment? So far as I know it still
commands the respect of the profession and the public, from
Lord Devlin at the summit to the individual in the street. All
the same some doubts begin to be expressed, and some abuses
plain. There has been widespread misuse of the right of
peremptory challenge, particularly in cases involving multiple
defendants, which has resulted in its reduction from a right to
challenge fifteen for each defendant to three, but not yet its
abolition. There have been repeated attempts, discovered
usually only in the cases in which they have failed, to intimi-
date or bribe jurors, so easily followed home or made the
subject of threatening telephone calls. There is the immense
problem of trying long cases of commercial frauds which may
run into months' duration. Not only is the evidence often
immensely technical, and extremely complex, but the mere
fact that members of a jury selected to try a case of this nature
must make themselves available for months of continuous
sitting during consecutive weeks precludes a random choice,
besides imposing great hardship on those unable to excuse
themselves. The American method of selection, involving
careful examination of personal backgrounds, is certainly

unattractive to an English practitioner, accustomed as he is to random selection. But is the comparison altogether to our advantage? Recent examples have been disclosed of persons sitting on juries with known criminal records, some with long strings of serious offences to their discredit. In one case which came to my knowledge, a defendant, ultimately convicted after, I think, more than one trial, had boasted before arraignment that no English jury would convict him. He had some reason for this boast. He had five previous acquittals on serious charges. He was either extremely unlucky in being falsely accused five times, or extremely lucky in his juries or perhaps it was not luck at all.

The strength of the jury system lies in the sense of responsibility of the average individual citizen where his own personal interests are not involved; the perfectly proper distrust of the public, and therefore of jurors, of persons in authority, including police, judges, counsel, public officials and experts; and the fact that each particular jury, once its period of service is over, never reassembles, and therefore can acquire no reputation for lenience or severity, or indeed bias of any kind. It remains, I am sure, in the field of criminal law at least, a popular institution, to interfere with which would cause widespread consternation. Nevertheless, false convictions as well as perverse acquittals do take place perhaps more often than is supposed (especially when the question is one of identity) and, unless there has been a misdirection on the part of the judge, or some other irregularity in the trial, they are almost impossible to upset, except in the unlikely event of the convicted person, like Adolph Beck in the early years of this century (but there are other and much more recent examples), actually being able to prove his innocence after all attempts at appeal have failed. Have we in the field of this venerated institution really evolved the most perfect system?

Would a reasoned judgment by a mixed court composed of laymen with a lawyer in the chair, combined, as it would have to be, with a wider right of appeal on fact, achieve less haphazard results? The difficulty with criminal law is that you cannot without good reason experiment with the liberties of human beings. Personally I would welcome an experiment on these lines limited to cases where the defendant consented and to the longer type of contested commercial fraud.

I cannot leave the jury system without a further word of criticism of my profession. Though they profess to venerate the jury, they do not trust it and the evidence is that they have never trusted it. The whole of the law of evidence, in some fields intact at the date of Miss Hamlyn's will, is replete with examples of this mistrust. Observe the best evidence rule, with its numerous exceptions, the hearsay rule with its different exceptions not less numerous, the careful protection of the character of the accused, fully justified in my opinion, the old Statute of Frauds and the section of the Sale of Goods Act derived from it (both now largely, but not quite, obsolete) requiring written evidence of certain kinds of contract signed by the person to be bound, and even the old rules governing the competence of witnesses, which prevented either Mrs. Bardell or Mr. Pickwick from giving evidence in their famous breach of promise case, or (prior to 1898) an accused defendant from giving evidence on his own behalf. All betray an underlying unwillingness to entrust juries with all the relevant material, or to believe that in emotionally charged issues they can distinguish truth from falsehood, or put prejudice and sentimentality out of their minds in favour of an objective approach to relevance or its opposite. There is something of a contrast, I believe, between the professed veneration of juries by their worshippers and their actual behaviour when confronted with the object of their worship. They are like fetish worshippers now adoring their idol, now distrusting it, now placing offerings on its altars, now seeking to placate it with incantations.

But does the profession and does Parliament trust the present standard method of trial by judge alone in civil cases any more than a jury? There is evidence to the contrary. This is to be found in the proliferation since the war of tribunals of all sorts outside the ordinary structure of the courts, not always involving the right to legal representation, nor the benefit of legal aid, and seldom bound by the strict rules of evidence or procedure. Typically these involve a legal chairman with two lay members, often drawn one from each side of organisations representing supposedly adverse economic or social groups. In origin, these tribunals were designed as alternatives to what was believed to be the artificial formality of courts of law, and the supposed ignorance of the ordinary judiciary of specialised information regarding particular economic and social relationships. The ordinary man or woman was expected to be able to operate the process without benefit of counsel or solicitors. It soon began to appear, however, that the total absence of formality could be a straightforward passport to injustice. Moreover, in rent cases, and cases of unfair dismissal, the landlord or employer could hardly be expected to spend long days in court instead of managing his own business, and therefore might reasonably be expected to employ a professional advocate. The first characteristic led to a widespread extension of the role of the ordinary courts in their supervisory role of subordinate tribunals, the second to an equally widespread demand for the extension of legal aid to tribunals originally instituted with the intention of keeping the lawyers out. One thing, however, has emerged from the development of the tribunal system since the war, and this is the marked preference shown by Parliament and the public for a tribunal consisting of a lawyer in the chair sitting with two seasoned and experienced lay members over trial by judge alone, or trial before a judge and civil jury. On advice, I endeavoured to give effect to the same principle in criminal cases in the new Crown Court set up by the Courts Act 1971, consisting when fully constituted of a judge and two magistrates. On appeals from magistrates in petty sessions and committals for sentence this appears to work fairly well, as it does with sentences in trials on indictment where a plea of guilty has been entered, and the two lay magistrates can sit with the judge and hear all the evidence. But where there is a contested jury case of any length the practical difficulties are formidable. The lay justices can play no part in the proceedings before the jury, but unless they have sat through the trial and heard the evidence, they cannot play any part in the sentencing process where their views would be most valuable.

During my first term of office I could not help noticing that the Committee on One Parent Families set up under the late Mr. Justice Finer proposed the setting up of a system of family courts, based on the same system, a judge in the chair and a layman on each side of him. If they had been set up it was proposed that they should take over the multifarious and often overlapping jurisdictions of magistrates' courts, county courts and the High Court in family and affiliation proceedings. So far, the scheme has proved too ambitious, perhaps too expensive, for immediate application, and contains individual features too numerous to make grafting easy on to existing structures.

I am left with a query in my mind. How far am I really satisfied with the present conception of "due process" as it has developed in the past 40 years, since Miss Hamlyn composed her will? The growth of administrative law and the development of the well-established if limited doctrine of natural

justice I regard as unqualified improvements. I am satisfied
with the almost complete elimination of the civil jury and
would myself have taken the process further. The criminal
jury, probably rightly, retains its popular approval as the
standard method of trial for serious crime, or at least the great
majority of such crimes. The proliferation of tribunals has, in
the main, justified itself. The new divorce laws still present
problems for the future. I believe Miss Hamlyn need have no
fear so far of the soundness in this field of her prescription.

Due Process Continued. The Judiciary

I end my examination with two questions which demand
attention. They both have to do with the role of the judiciary
as a separate arm of government. Are its limitations adequately understood? Is its integrity sufficiently guaranteed?

At the end of the long struggle between Parliament and the
Crown, Parliament had emerged as the victor by virtue of its
power to grant and withhold Supply and its legislative
authority. Every schoolboy knows this. But at that date the
power of the Crown was limited, not destroyed. William III
and Queen Anne were monarchs in fact as well as in name,
and, very soon afterwards, Montesquieu was able to divide
government into the classic three branches, executive, legislature, and judiciary, a pattern which was revived as the true
orthodoxy by the founding fathers of the American constitution. It was only under the Hanoverians that the executive and
the legislature gradually became fused, the former at first
controlling the latter by patronage and management, and
latterly by the slow democratisation of the constitution. This
left the judiciary out on a limb, by far the smallest and most
vulnerable arm of government, despite the nominal security
of tenure guaranteed by the Bill of Rights and the Act of

Settlement. In some ways their powers have since decreased. Originally their salaries were supposed to be sacrosanct, being paid directly from the Consolidated Fund. In my lifetime, inflation has ended all this, since judges' salaries diminish regularly with the value of money and, even in the case of the highest judiciary, until recently might be increased only by affirmative resolution of both Houses. Every time such a resolution was proposed and even now every time a Government decision is announced on the latest report of the Top Salaries Review Body, the conduct, social background, and impartiality of the judges are made the subject of highly unedifying controversy and debate both in Parliament and in the Press. A book by a professor has been written on the subject. Whilst debate must be free, the consequences have been serious, since the freedom of every country depends as much on the independence, impartiality and integrity of the judiciary as upon parliamentary government, the freedom of the Press and the universality of the franchise. In one way or another this is recognised in every civilised country.

But I find that this vital consideration is not always observed in practice. I believe it to be true that throughout my adult life promotion to the judiciary from the practising profession has been based on merit, and directly political appointments have gradually ceased and are now virtually unknown. This of course does not mean that judges are, in the wider sense, immune from political pressures. I know of one High Court judge, now deceased, who, I believe, would be alive today had he not been subjected to a torrent of abuse excited by the media against a decision, which, though varied on appeal, was none the less subsequently endorsed in principle. I am not the only one who holds the belief that this sensitive man was, almost literally, hounded by the media to his grave. Though I could not prove it, I know of two mem-

bers of the higher judiciary whose career prospects were
substantially delayed by reason of directly political considera-
tions. There is, of course, the constant and popular clamour
for public inquiries whenever anything goes wrong in public
life, and, when this happens, all too often the Lord Chancellor
is asked to find a High Court judge to head it even though the
inquisitorial method involved is somewhat alien to his experience, and the political sensitivity of the issues only too
manifest. I do my best to avoid using judges for this purpose.
But, after the so-called Bloody Sunday in Belfast, I was only
too well aware that an English High Court judge would be
required to head a Tribunal of Inquiry, and I reached the
extremely distasteful conclusion that the only figure in public
life adequate in stature to discharge the task was the then Lord
Chief Justice of England himself. Though he carried through
the disagreeable task with admirable impartiality, a foolish
and biased American academic subjected his conclusions to
ignorant and insulting criticism. I fear that, after Brixton,
Lord Scarman (whom again I persuaded to preside over the
inevitable inquiry) may find his reputation irremediably
affected by political criticism or admiration, despite his impec-
cable and sensitive behaviour and his wholly impartial report.
To a distinguished member of the Bar whom I persuaded to
chair another, and emotionally charged, inquiry I thought it
right to issue an unequivocal warning that his chances of
elevation to the Bench might, in certain circumstances, be
compromised. Honourably, he disregarded my warning,
which, as matters turned out, was unnecessary.

The 400 odd Circuit judges and stipendiary magistrates
undertake their judicial careers entirely on the recommenda-
tion of the Lord Chancellor of the day, and do not enjoy, at
least in theory, the protection conferred by the Bill of Rights
and the Act of Settlement, for, since the Lord Chancellor can

dismiss them for misbehaviour or incapacity, and the Lord Chancellor is responsible to Parliament, their continuance in office can, at least in theory, be made the subject of political pressure. I have no doubt, myself, that such pressure, when brought to bear, is misconceived. The phrases "misbehaviour" and "incapacity" are, I believe, capable of interpretation by the courts, and I myself have no doubt that, if the Lord Chancellor attempted to exercise his powers of removal without strict adherence to the rules of natural justice, or if he gave the phrases "misbehaviour" or "incapacity" a meaning more extensive than they can legitimately bear, he could find himself challenged by his victim in an application for judicial review in the Divisional Court of the Queen's Bench Division. Nevertheless, the power of removal exists, and in practice this means that questions can be raised in the House of Commons, and resolutions passed in less formal organisations demanding its use, when the decision of a case by a Circuit judge or below attracts popular attention, or proves controversial, or even when an *obiter dictum*, whether in context or out of it, appears harsh, unduly lenient, or merely absurd. It is idle to pretend that such questions or such resolutions, duly reported in the Press, cannot, at least potentially, threaten judicial independence, and the events to which I made reference a few moments ago clearly establish that the often quoted remark by Lord Salmon, that a judge who minds criticism in the Press or in Parliament is not worthy of a place on the Bench, was, to say the least, a trifle optimistic, even if not actually lacking in realism.

In some ways, the power and influence of judges is greater than it was in 1932 when I first went to the Bar. The virtual abolition of the civil jury to which I have already referred has put much greater power in the hands of the judge of first instance, and though, unlike a jury, he must give reasons for his decision, and is therefore subject to appeal, an appellate court is extremely slow to question his soundness on matters of fact when he has seen the witnesses and they have not. In matters of discretion his powers are even less easily questioned. The direct application of parts of the European Treaties, to which all courts, whether of first instance or appellate, must give direct effect, is another step in the same direction. Either by direct application, or by reference to the European Court under Article 177 of the EEC Treaty and the corresponding Articles of the other European Treaties, judges are much freer in matters to which the Treaties apply to criticise Acts of Parliament or secondary legislation than at any time since the beginning of the eighteenth century. I have already referred to their increasingly interventionist policy towards Ministers and local authority which has inevitably raised the question, mainly posed by left wing politicians, of the role in society which judges ought to be permitted to play. I have already referred to the danger that the increasing passion of the public for "wide ranging public inquiries," with a High Court judge in the chair, or worse still, sitting alone, however flattering they may be to the general reputation of the judiciary for impartiality, may invest particular judges with a politically coloured aura or persona. These are not necessarily healthy signs.

It might be supposed from what I have said that in this dispute I am heart and soul in support of the judiciary against the politician. That, of course, is fully in accordance with the duty of a Lord Chancellor. But it would be strange if, with experience of seven years of judges and judgments behind me as Lord Chancellor, it were the whole truth, and it is not the whole truth. I simply do not echo wholeheartedly the words of a recent member of the Court of Appeal "trust the judges" any more than I echo the hostile question raised often in the media and by left wing academics and members of the House of Commons in the form: "Are the judges to be trusted?" with the clear implication that they form part of an inherently right-wing establishment, whose bias is all the more dangerous because it is unconscious. I have already paid my tribute to the increasingly creative and constructive role played by the judiciary since 1945 in the control of the executive and the vindication of individual rights against authority in its various forms and misuse of power by private corporations, associations or unions. That is precisely what an independent judiciary is for in an age of social and economic change. The rule of law is not static but dynamic, and T. S. Eliot's witticism to the effect that the lawyer's motto must always be: "The spirit killeth, the letter giveth life" is at best only partly true. On the other side of the coin it is necessary to realise the limitation of the judicial role. The law has its discipline. It must never become the thing which seems right in the eye of the individual judge. It is not as long as the judge's foot, and this limitation is as much there, though of course less obviously so, in the case of customary or common law as in the case of obedience to an Act of Parliament. "Be you never so high but the law is above you" is a rule for judges no less than Ministers, and, if the independence of judges is to be preserved, the limitations on the judicial function must be clearly understood not only by the public and the media, but by the judiciary themselves, both collectively and individually.

I cast aside as unscholarly, superficial and worthless recent analyses imputing political attitudes to the judiciary based on parentage, family background and education. Apart from the fact that all are of necessity out of date since at best the judiciary represent the social and educational system 40 years or so before their appointment (and one writer at least has gone back in his analyses before 1914) the fact is that, unlike jurors, judges can never be a random sample of the community. All over the world, professional judges must be recruited from graduates, and in future, the great majority, unlike their predecessors, will have been trained in law to the exclusion of any other discipline. This is as true of Moscow, Paris, or New York, as it is of London.

I also regard with a degree of indifference verging on contempt the criticism of judges that demands for them a type of training which would render them more like assessors or expert witnesses than judges of fact and law. I personally regret the partial elimination of the lawyer with a good general education culminating in a degree gained in a subject other than law. Lord Wilberforce, one of the best judges I have ever known, received the old classical education culminating in a double first at Oxford in Honour Mods and Greats before he read a word of law. Lord Diplock read chemistry at Oxford, with the language of which he is still sufficiently familiar to be able to hear patent appeals. Lord Denning got a first in mathematics in addition to his first in law. Though he had a good academic mind, my father gradu- ated to the Woolsack by way of growing sugar in British Guiana, serving as a trooper in the South African War, and as a solicitor's clerk with Ashurst, Morris and Crisp. I believe all these to have become better lawyers and, in due course, better judges because and not in spite of these wider ex- periences. Lord Birkenhead is, I believe, the only Lord Chan- cellor to have achieved a first class degree at Oxford in the Honours school of jurisprudence. Lord Gardiner studied law at Oxford, but is said to have achieved a fourth class, and the first Lord Dilhorne a third. In the formative years of the common law there was no law degree to be had at an English university at all. This does not mean that I underrate law as an academic study. Quite the contrary, and, as will be seen, the contrary is true. The point I am about to make is a different one. Whether they are law graduates or not I have always advised aspiring practitioners to take their academic course in law extremely seriously, but not at the expense of their general reading and education. What I am attacking is not at all a general training in academic subjects or in the so-called university of life as a preliminary to legal practice or judicial office, but the ignorant clamour that is sometimes heard that judges should be made to undergo some specialised training in some such subject as say psychology, sociology, forensic medicine, or even mechanical engineering or accountancy as a preliminary to their appointment as judges. It is doubtless true that they are likely to try cases in which familiarity with one or more of such specialist subjects is likely to prove useful. But the range of such subjects is potentially so wide as to make a specialised study of a quarter of them impracticable, and the only effect of attempting to add a specific course in any of them on to the training of judges would be to make its graduates only too prone to substitute their own learning for their true function. The judge's function is to listen intelligently and patiently to evidence and argument using rival expert witnesses where specialised knowledge is required, to identify the right points, to evaluate the reliability and relevance of oral testimony, and draw the right inference from primary fact, and finally to reach a conclusion based on an accurate knowledge of law and practice. A judge must be able to diagnose pretentiousness. He must learn to discern the difference between honest error and fraud. The capacity of being a judge is acquired in the course of practising the law, interviewing clients or expert witnesses, hearing and examining witnesses in court, watching experienced judges at work, and above all in advising others, after reading, analysing and reflecting on the relevant material. It is, of course, an advantage to know something of medicine, science and mathematics, and to have moved knowledgeably in the wider world of society and literature. But it is not the business of a judge to act as an expert in any field but his own. In addition to knowledge and experience the qualities he brings to his work are the ability to make up his mind when the case is complete, and the ability not to make it up until everyone has had his legitimate say.

The limitations which judges and others must accept are that judges should only be employed and should only express opinions upon matters which are both justiciable and properly before them. If they are employed outside this field they are embarking upon an unknown territory, and, if they generalise on matters not properly before them, they bring the profession of a judge into deserved criticism.

On the whole the public spirit amongst judges will lead them at least to attempt the task which they are asked to perform, however unsuitable. They have been employed to investigate the Profumo affair and its repercussions, the events of "Bloody Sunday," miners' wages, the role of the police, methods of police discipline, immigration, and riots. So long as these questions revolve around a disputed issue of what actually happened in a given case there can in principle be no objection to employing judges in an enterprise of this kind, though in the nature of the case the method of an inquiry is intrinsically inquisitorial, while the techniques with which judges are more familiar are essentially adversarial, and there must be present at the time the inquiry is instituted all the conditions which render an inquiry suitable. (Some of these were absent in the Denning inquiry into the rumours arising out of the Profumo affair, and others were absent in the Croom-Johnson inquiry into the Crown Agents.) But where the issue begins and ends as one of policy, like miners' wages, or the role of the police, it is surely wrong to employ judges at all, notwithstanding their known impartiality and the ability which most judges possess of making tolerably good chairmen. Judges are not ordinarily good judges of policy, and questions of policy are not ordinarily justiciable in the sense of the word I have defined. Judges are not to be blamed for their public spirit in accepting commissions of this kind. But the media, public opinion, politicians, and I fear Lord Chancellors, not least myself, are possibly to be criticised for asking judges to perform tasks for which their training does not render them particularly suitable, and which, potentially at least, do interfere with their ordinary work and add a political flavour to their reputation.

If judges are innocent, and even praiseworthy, in accepting tasks to which for one reason or another they are unsuited, or which ought not to be attempted at all, they are less free from blame when they succumb to the temptation to generalise about matters not strictly germane to the subject-matter before them. Every judge succumbs to this temptation from time to time. After all they are only human, and part of their ordinary task is to deal with subjects highly charged with emotion, or highly sensitive politically, such as sexual conduct, sentencing policy, race relations, the policy underlying Acts of Parliament or subordinate legislation, the characteristics of well-known personalities, and trade unions. Even without superfluous dicta the mere performance of his duty will give a judge trouble enough. It is inevitable that, in dealing with cases before him, a judge will have to come to hard, unpopular, and in any case controversial, decisions for which he is bound to give reasons. By the mere process of decision he cannot avoid the natural growth and withering away of legal doctrine. He cannot select the cases which come

before him. He cannot decline to decide them in favour of one
party or the other. If he moves a little further along the line of
decided cases he extends the law available to a later judge who
has to decide another case in a related or analogous field. But
he develops the law no less if he thinks that decided cases have
already gone far enough along a particular line and thus
restricts a principle from further extension. If he tries to define
the purpose of an enactment, which may not be very clearly
stated, and to give effect to it, he may widen the canons for the
interpretation of statutes. He will narrow them every time he
declines to adopt this course, and narrowly interprets the
printed word according to its grammatical sense. If he prides
himself on putting justice, or what he regards as justice, in
front of received legal doctrine, he is in danger of substituting
subjective criteria for consistency, where certainty in the law
may be the overriding requirement. If he sticks pedantically to
precedent he may easily fall into the trap of producing logical
or jurisprudential absurdity, countenancing oppression and
fraud, or leaving the injured party without a remedy at law. If
he goes beyond it, he usurps legislative power. Thus in any
event his responsibilities are great. But he is usually wise to
stick to the particular even when he is being at his most
creative, and to observe the fiction that he is only interpreting
and systematising existing law when he is fully aware that, by
his decision, he cannot avoid breaking new ground.

May I draw my threads of argument together? Judicial
independence is the secret of the reputation justly held by
British justice. The achievement of judicial independence at
the end of the seventeenth century, enshrined in the Bill of
Rights and the Act of Settlement, is just as important a
landmark in the history of liberty under law as the victory of
Parliament over the Crown, and is not adequately recognised
as such. It depends on security of tenure for the judges and

immunity from attack either by Parliament or the executive or from the media. By itself the jury is not sufficient guarantee of such liberty. Before judicial independence, juries were manipulated. Juries can be packed, either by manipulating the panel, or improper and concerted use of the power of challenge. Jurors can be bribed or intimidated by criminal interference, which is happening now on a scale until recently not generally appreciated. This, more even than the danger of communal voting, was the danger which brought about the establishment of the Diplock Courts in Northern Ireland. The real safeguard of the subject is judicial independence, and here is where the second part of Miss Hamlyn's injunction must be respected. Judges are human and subject to human error and human frailty. But they have a difficult, embarrassing and occasionally odious task, which may involve harsh statements, the imposition of serious penalties, or the adoption of unpopular and unpalatable decisions. It is only if public opinion, or, as Miss Hamlyn's will had it, the Common People of this United Kingdom, realise how unusual a privilege it is to live under a system of law administered by impartial and incorruptible judges, and recognise the duty of upholding the impartiality and independence of the law by their constant support against all-comers, that it will be preserved here into the twenty-first century. Of this responsibility a heavy share must be taken by the legal profession as a whole, partly because it is only from an incorrupt and independent legal profession that judges possessing the necessary qualities can be recruited, and partly because they are so placed as to be capable of understanding the importance of the point and provide the necessary leadership and impetus to keep the public steady and vigorous on the right course in an age of increasing violence and political encroachment.

Fifth Shock:
From Contract to Status

If I have understood Miss Hamlyn's thought correctly, she was probably unaware of Maine's dictum to the effect that the evolution of law from primitive forms to sophisticated and articulated codes was everywhere one from status to contract. Nevertheless, unless I have mistaken her, whether or not she was aware of it, her thinking was very largely guided by approval of the social and political processes which gave rise to his thinking. Obviously it was always a very broad generalisation, and one, therefore, which required a good deal of discussion and refinement to make it acceptable even at the time when it was printed. Nonetheless, at the time it was made, it was a shrewd and percipient assessment of a secular movement in legislation and law.

It would be less convincing if repeated now. Ever since the 1860s the movement has been strongly in the opposite direction, that is from contract to status, and in no part of this period has this movement been more apparent than in the 40 years since 1941. In their different ways my predecessors as Hamlyn lecturers have more or less unconsciously illustrated the point.

In the most recent series of all, Professor Honoré illustrates
the point as well as any. In the three or four different human
relationships with which he was concerned freedom of contract had been thought hitherto to reign almost supreme. But,
as Professor Honoré's analysis shows, the legal rights of the
parties have instead come to be developed by Parliament
increasingly in terms rather of status in which legal rights have
played an increasingly important part, and, to the extent that
they have, this status has overridden the terms of any contractual bargain between the parties. One such relationship is that
of landlord and tenant. Business tenancies, agricultural tenancies, and rent restricted and regulated residential tenancies
are no longer simply governed by terms freely negotiated. For
the most part contracting out is restricted or forbidden.
Legislation in this field, at first rather tentative, dates from the
1880s. But ever since the end of the First World War these
comparatively humble beginnings have developed to the
point where the statutory terms, designed to benefit the
tenant from the superior bargaining power of the landlord
where vacant accommodation is at a premium or the need for
continued security of tenure by the tenant weakens his
negotiating position, far outweigh in importance the mere
contractual terms of the tenancy in the relationship between
the parties. Business tenants have the right to a new lease,
indefinitely renewable. Agricultural tenants can be turned out
only on very limited grounds, and their holdings are heritable.
All except the most expensive lettings of either unfurnished or
furnished accommodation are regulated, both as to the
circumstances in which possession can be recovered and as to
other terms, including, in particular, rent. It is not part of my
intention to argue whether these changes are in the public
interest. There are some who argue that they contribute to
shortage of accommodation in fields where the Acts apply. I

simply point to the fact that the changes have taken place, and that Parliament has progressively imposed a position approximating to status where freedom of contract has previously prevailed. It has done so in the interest of the party whom it conceives to be in the weaker bargaining position.

A second, and similar, relationship expounded by Professor Honoré is that between employer and employed. Here again the effect of legislation has been to restrict freedom of contract in the interest of what Parliament rightly or wrongly has judged to be the weaker party. Already, in the nineteenth century, Lord Shaftesbury had been campaigning successfully for the protection of women and children in factories and mines. There are very few fields of employment contract into which Parliament has not inserted statutory terms and prohibitions, almost all in favour of the employee, each time substituting inalienable rights in place of freely negotiated terms. These affect the right to a written contract, the duration of the employment, restrictions on dismissal, redundancy payments, rights to trade union activities, industrial injuries benefits, and countless other restrictions and duties as regards safety and conditions of work.

A third field dealt with by Professor Honoré is, of course, more contentious. This is the field of marriage and its consequences. Civil marriage has always been a contract leading to a status. The element of status is, in fact, inherent in the very idea of marriage in any sort of society whatever. At first sight it might appear that the progressive relaxation of the bond constituting the status which has continuously evolved since 1857 is essentially a movement away from status in the direction of contract. I would argue that this is not the case, especially since 1969 when fault ceased to be the basis for the dissolution of a marriage which had irretrievably broken down. Apart from the vastly increased number of persons who have been given licence to remarry by the grant of a decree absolute for dissolution, what in fact has happened has been that instead of ending on dissolution the relationship between the former spouses has been increasingly regulated by the courts. These have wide powers to redistribute property, to vary, increase, or reduce maintenance, to deal with custody, care and control, and access to children. The status created by dissolution of a former marriage can pursue the parties through the rest of their lives, all too frequently in an atmosphere of increasing bitterness, in many cases accompanied by considerable hardship on both sides, and, where children are involved, to their lasting psychological detriment. Again, it is not my present intention to argue the merits of this policy. I simply point to the fact that increasing numbers of persons, the parties to, and the children of, former marriages have their incomes and property investigated and ultimately distributed by the courts without their being able to contract out of the obligations which the courts are bound to define, and, in default, enforce.

Lord Scarman and others have pointed to the international factors introduced by our adhesion to the European Convention on Human Rights, even though, as has happened, Parliament has hitherto declined to embody these rights, or any other human rights, in our municipal law. Viewed as a tendency in our jurisprudence this, too, can be seen as a move towards a series of rights entrenched for the benefit of the individual in the direction of status and against the overweening power of modern bureaucracy, a powerful corporation or a union.

But, of course, by far the most important development of status legislation has been the gradual erection of the Welfare State itself. Though its foundations, of course, date from the Liberal Governments of 1906 to 1914, and even earlier, the present form which this takes derives from the enactments of the Labour Government of 1945 to 1950. These broadly gave effect to the main provisions of the Beveridge Report of 1942. The various benefits to be obtained from what used to be called the stamp, and its supplement from the general product of taxation, have really conferred what is in fact a status on every individual subject. This status is embodied in secondary legislation of immense complexity, but equally of immense value. The total effect and purpose of this legislation is to confer on the individual security from the worst effects of poverty, disease and old age. Coupled with the vastly improved provision for education under the Education Act 1944 this complex bundle of rights has completely altered the position of the individual. Again, I am not primarily arguing the political pros and cons. The fact is that irreversible changes of immense magnitude have taken place over the 40 years under discussion. Previous Hamlyn lecturers have drawn attention to these changes. The discussion of these is surely part of the functions of Miss Hamlyn's lecturer. They form an indefeasible part of the privileges of British citizenship and the responsibilities attaching to it. In each case however the effect is to confer status and to reduce the field in which the individual is dependent on contract or personal effort to govern his standard of life.

Some of these responsibilities have also assumed a less agreeable statutory form in the immensely increased complexity, and weight, of the burden of taxation which has been the inevitable complement of the development of the British State during the past 40 years. So far as concerned direct taxation by central government this was illustrated by Mr. Hubert Munroe in his recent series of Hamlyn lectures. But the whole burden of taxation direct and indirect including local authority rates and V.A.T. is also involved. Attempts have been made to reduce this burden or even to reduce the rate of increase, including those made under the present administration. But, despite promises of tax relief and much talk of spending cuts, and endless wailing and gnashing of teeth, public expenditure has continued to rise, both absolutely and as a proportion of Gross Domestic Product. We spend currently some £120,000 million a year, and are adding to our borrowing at an annual rate of £10,000 million a year. In the last decade or so, the national borrowing has more than trebled, and with it the servicing of debt at what, in the comparatively recent past, would have been regarded as exorbitant rates of interest, so that, unless social security payments have been lumped together, the servicing of previous debt has become the largest single item in public expenditure. I do not propose in any detail to handle what is obviously a topic too controversial politically for Miss Hamlyn's lecturer. But there are two facts so obvious that even in the present context they cannot be omitted. The first is that, for whatever other purpose borrowing may be justified, it is not possible, and by this I mean literally not possible, to go on borrowing indefinitely to meet the service of debt previously incurred. The second is that almost the whole of the political pressure on successive governments, of whatever political colour, comes from single purpose pressure groups and from general purpose parties and organisations whose sole object in life is to induce Government and local authorities to spend more money in one department or another. The arguments in support of such demands are always compelling. It may be the needs of the Third World, or of the old, or the young or the sick, or defence, or law and order, or the need to reduce unemployment by subsidised public expenditure, or to invest money in capital projects. In each case the effect is to increase the total burden of public expenditure, and with it to subordinate the part which the individual can play of his own volition to control his destiny. We have developed political institutions with increased powers over the individual, but find ourselves less and less able to control demands based on open-ended requirements of potentially infinite size. A state so orientated is embarked on a course bound sooner or later to lead to economic and personal subordination, in short the diminution of freedom under the rule of law which is after all the very thing which Miss Hamlyn wished her lecturers to defend. Whatever other lessons one is expected to draw from this, they must include the proposition that if it is, indeed, a privilege to be British in these latter days, the responsibilities imposed upon those who enjoy these privileges do not diminish with time but must include a responsibility to insist on some constraints on expenditure. I am not less, but rather the more, dismayed by the comparison which Miss Hamlyn invites me to make with other similarly placed communities. If I were to make such comparisons it would appear that similar forces are at work throughout the world from the United States to the Iron Curtain and beyond. It is a mistake to suppose that any country, Communist or free, North or South, undeveloped or industrialised, is immune from the tendencies of instability brought about by the inclination of rulers to spend beyond their means. Often they then compound their guilt by putting the blame on others who are not in a position to influence their course of action.

I must, however, return to the main line of my argument. The vast increase in state activity to which I have been drawing attention all along obviously sets problems for the judiciary and for the legal profession. The whole apparatus of the Welfare State is, of course, constantly giving rise to disputes between the individual and the authorities which administer different fields of state activity, from the tribunals administering redundancy payments and unfair dismissals to the social security commissioners. It would, I suppose, have been possible to graft all these systems on to the existing pyramid of courts of first instance, with provision for appeal to the Court of Appeal and the House of Lords. I could not help fancying, rightly or wrongly, that, in the end, this was the structure which Lord Scarman would have preferred, or, perhaps, would still prefer. Whether or not I am correct in this, it has not been the course followed, and, in any event, if this be his view I do not think that I agree with it. Granted that the encroachment by politicians and the media on the judicial function gives some cause for some disquiet, I do not think the balance is at all redressed by giving the judges the right of decision in purely administrative or policy questions for which their training and experience do not necessarily suit them well. Granted that the rule of law demands that the courts must always retain jurisdiction to curb misbehaviour or oppression by subordinate bodies of all kinds, administrative, judicial, executive, or even, like local authorities, those entrusted with subordinate legislative functions, it by no means follows that they should undertake the performance of the functions with which these bodies have been properly endowed, or decide the matters which are entrusted to their judgment. The function of the courts can be adequately performed if judges are limited to judicial review of *ultra vires,* unfair, interested, or manifestly perverse decisions by subordinate authority, or, in the case of purely legal questions, an appellate function.

The last matter raised by the movement in our institutions which I have been examining in this series is that of the interpretation and drafting of statute. This has come more and more to the fore as a matter for discussion in recent years. As long ago as 1969 the Law Commission produced a draft Bill which has so far, even as Lord Scarman has endeavoured to modify it, failed to receive parliamentary endorsement. Mr. Francis Bennion, a former parliamentary draftsman, has written learnedly upon it. Lord Renton chaired a committee on the subject which reported, and some of whose recommendations have been adopted. Lord Renton continues to pursue the remainder with admirable persistence from his place in Parliament. Lord Denning has produced a number of views from time to time, both from the Bench and in public utterance. Sir William Dale, like Mr. Bennion with some actual experience of parliamentary draftsmanship, has written a fascinating volume comparing our own drafting techniques with those of Sweden, France, and Western Germany, and has reached the undeniable but remarkable conclusion that our own legislative practice achieves Bills varying between twice, three or even five times as long as those of our Western European neighbours, without adding significantly to the content. This at least is partly borne out by my own experience. During my first term of office as Lord Chancellor I was entertained in Paris most hospitably by my opposite number M. Pleven, the French Garde des Sceaux. M. Pleven then showed me his *projet de loi* for the French legal aid scheme (approximately the same as our civil legal aid) which contained only about one-third of the bulk of our comparable British statute. The importance of this subject is demonstrated both by the growing bulk of our statute law, and by the consequential fact that (I would guess) over nine out of ten cases heard on appeal before either the Court of Appeal or the House of Lords either turn upon, or involve, the meaning of words contained in enactments of primary or secondary legislation.

The kernel of the problem lies in the fact that there is no effective canon applicable in all cases to the construction of statute, and that there is no effective definition of what may or may not be referred to or read in court or studied in private reading by the judge as a guide to the elucidation of the meaning which Parliament intended to convey by the words it used. It is common ground, of course, that a textbook by a deceased writer with legal qualifications can be referred to in court as a persuasive authority, and that living writers may be read in court as encapsulating the argument of counsel, or for the purpose of formulating propositions from which he means to dissent. It is equally common ground that, for certain limited purposes, Blue Books are not always out of bounds, but that *Hansard* always is. It is by no means apparent, however, to what extent a judge may indulge in private reading not referred to in court, either in his preliminary researches or in composing a judgment, and what happens when he has done so either by accident or by design, and thus stumbled on material which could not be used by counsel, but which may affect his mind. This is largely uncharted territory and, without citing authority which in this series, in the interest of the "Common People" referred to in my remit, I have rather forsworn, I have the impression that the law is somewhat more fluid and flexible than judicial utterances occasionally suggest.

On the surface the problem revolves round the centuries-old dispute between the mischievites (founding on Lord Coke), the literalists (who, on paper at least, have largely won the field), the purposivists (as the neo-mischievites like to think of themselves), and the followers of the "golden rule" who seek to find an uncomfortable accommodation between the rival schools. As Lord Renton observes, the different principles are, or may prove, inconsistent in practice. It is common ground that the judges are bound to carry out the intentions of Parliament, once these have been ascertained.

But how may the wishes of Parliament be discerned? I myself do not find quite the difficulty sometimes urged. It is obvious of course that, if Parliament expresses itself plainly enough in language which is capable of only one meaning, there is only one interpretation open to the courts. This is the decisive factor which has led to the virtual triumph of the literalist school. Lord Coke's formulation of the "mischief" principle was based on a theory of statute law as merely corrective of or supplementary to common law which no longer corresponds to fact. But there are no words in any document which must not be read in context, and whose meaning does not vary to some extent with the context in which they are to be read. In the immensely complex jungle of statute law it would be an imprudent judge who did not take into account the main legislative purpose of an Act, and the political and social context in which it was passed. To give an obvious example, if Parliament chooses to pass in an unaltered form a draft Bill proposed by the Law Commission, it would be an act of folly in cases of difficulty not to read the report on which the draft was based or the commentary on the draft which commonly accompanies this report. Equally, it is reasonable that in imposing a new charge of tax or restricting the liberty of the subject, Parliament would expect the courts to take a fairly restrictive, though, as the recent *Rossminster* decision shows, not necessarily an artificial, view of the extent of the restriction or the new impost intended. Equally, laws intended to protect the weak against the strong in cases where their vulnerable position makes them the weaker party in negotiation can well be given a liberal interpretation which would be inappropriate in taxing statutes. I have already referred to this in discussing legislation giving statutory rights to master and servant or landlord and tenant. But this is no new doctrine. Since *Groves* v. *Wimborne*, almost the whole of the jurisprudence which has revolutionised the jurisdiction in tort in claims for damages for personal injury derives from the deliberate policy of the courts to give a right of action for damages for breach of statutory duty where Parliament had purported to impose only a penalty. When judges decline to "read words into" an Act of Parliament which are not there they would do well to reflect on the implications of *Groves* v. *Wimborne* and the immense and beneficial consequences which have flowed from it.

There is therefore nothing necessarily arbitrary or improper if judges select a restricted or extended interpretation of an Act based less on language than the nature and purpose of the legislation. Of course nothing could be more "inconsistent" than the two principles. Extended and restricted principles of construction are, of course, direct opposites. But though admittedly the adoption of the one principle and not the other proceeds well beyond the literal or grammatical interpretation of the language employed there is nothing intrinsically irrational or arbitrary about it. I once took part in the hearing of an appeal in the House of Lords in which both counsel and at least one member of the appellate committee had actually participated in the production of a report which had given rise to the Act of Parliament whose interpretation was under discussion. What could be more artificial than to refuse to look at the Blue Book? This contained an accurate summary of the pre-existing law, as good as could be provided in any legal textbook, a full discussion of the merits and demerits of various proposals for change, and a series of recommendations some of which obviously had, and some of which obviously had not, been incorporated into the Act, together with other provisions which must have owed their origin to the legislative or prelegislative procedures themselves. I know at least one distinguished Law Lord (now retired) who actually told me that he saw no reason at all why, equally, *Hansard* should not be consulted as a guide to the interpretation of statute. But I did not and do not agree with him. The reasons are both constitutional and practical. From the practical point of view, I do not myself see how the collective will of Parliament, as a Bill plods its way through both Houses, can be discerned from individual speeches from different quarters at different hours of the day, saying different things to a shifting audience of varying size. From the constitutional viewpoint, I do not think it appropriate with a view to the comity between the different branches of Government, and their independence of each from the other, that the actual proceedings in Parliament should be the subject of discussion (and thereby inevitably criticism) in the courts both from the Bench and by counsel. What was said by a Minister or private member at two o'clock in the morning in the course of a report stage on a hot June night is more likely to mislead than enlighten, and criticism of it by judges, which would not only be legitimate but necessary were it to be admissible, would be constitutionally most undesirable. This does not mean that, in their private reading, either counsel or judges should restrict themselves in any way from exposure to the normal currents of public discussion. All that is said in public can be used as background material by those with access to it, and the inclination to digest it. A judge who is impressed by a point picked up in private reading should of course put it before counsel to enable them to deal with it, and counsel must argue any such point of which he desires to make use without referring to the source.

I seem to have strayed some way from my original thesis. I was originally concerned to point out that, in the 40 years I have selected for review, statute law, with a complex network of social policies and rights, has assumed a vastly increased importance as against the old common law rules of contract, or, for that matter, tort and crime. This development has inevitably raised new problems in judicial administration, and greatly accentuated the need for fresh thinking about the draftsmanship and interpretation of statutes. What it has not done, at least in my view, is to invalidate any part of Miss Hamlyn's general thesis about the value of our institutions. These have worn well. They have not remained static. In itself that is an advantage. The changes only emphasise both parts of her contention, first that it is a privilege to live in this country, and second, that if it is desired to retain the privilege, it is necessary to recognise a special responsibility on those who enjoy it.

Sixth Shock:
Law and Order

Lord Chancellors are expected to remain silent on crime. This is because crime, and criminal procedure, are regarded as the responsibility of the Home Secretary, and Home Secretaries jealously invigilate the frontiers which separate their province from that occupied by their legal colleagues on the Woolsack.

There are, however, a few topics in this field which it must be proper to explore. Over the whole of my career at the Bar, crime and criminal law have assumed greater and greater importance. My father used to boast that, until he became Attorney-General, he had engaged, I believe, in only three criminal proceedings. Neither he nor any one else at the time considered this limitation on his experience a disadvantage. It would be hard to find a common lawyer who could really say the same today. The causes are threefold, the vast increase in the number and types of conduct which may give rise to criminal prosecution, the actual increase in crime, and the development of criminal legal aid. In her return journey across the Styx Miss Hamlyn's shade will require reassurance on all these topics.

Despite all temptations, I do not propose to discuss

generally the subject of criminal penalties. If I am right in picturing her as a lady of conservative outlook (with a small "c"), I doubt whether Miss Hamlyn would have approved the abolition of the death penalty for murder, and perhaps not even the abolition of corporal punishment. The fact remains that, since 1948, no House of Commons, on a free vote, has been prepared to sanction either, and I rather agree with those who think that, whatever the merits, neither topic is particularly appropriate material for a three-line whip. Whilst I am myself apprehensive that the total abolition of the death penalty may have afforded an actual incentive to murder in a limited range of instances, I do not think I could justify the belief that it is, in general, responsible for the exponential rise in crimes of violence (still less for the rise in other types of crime) which has taken place over the last 40 years. I am not sure that I could put my finger on a single cause. Nevertheless, like almost everyone else, I am profoundly dismayed by the extent to which violence has increased, and, in particular, by the extent to which even otherwise civilised persons seem to tolerate it as a means of drawing attention to political or social grievances. I do not myself believe that murder, maiming, or torture is any less horrific because it is inspired by political motivation. On the contrary, I regard political motivation in general as an aggravating, and not a mitigating, factor in assessing the seriousness of violent crime. Law and order I regard as a seamless robe. You cannot tear one part of the fabric without doing damage to the whole. The objective of the lawgiver should be so far as possible to limit the imposition of obligations and restrictions to actions or omissions which can be justified as morally requisite or blameworthy irrespective of criminal sanction, and to provide means of change open to those dissatisfied with the status quo which offer reasonable prospects of achieving legitimate objectives by constitutional means. If the rule of law does not comply with this requirement, of course it encourages unilateral action, and unilateral action outside the law inevitably involves or leads to violence of one sort or another. In a free society the individual must accept the authority of law as he finds it, and not defy it without overwhelming reason.

However, in one way or another, we are living in a wave of violence throughout the world, which I can only ascribe to a widespread weakening in the respect for moral values, and political and social authority, without which ordered society is impossible. I am not much reassured by the comparison which my instructions literally interpreted would compel me to make with Amsterdam, Paris, Rome, Western Germany, Chicago or New York. The problem seems worse there than it is in London. But that does not diminish the seriousness of what is happening here. Whilst I am not denying the relevance of social conditions generally, I am not wholly convinced by sociological explanations of criminal activity which cite bad housing, poor employment prospects, racial or religious discrimination, or poor education as causes of it. I have never known periods of my life when education or housing has been better than now, and I can remember times when unemployment and employment prospects were much worse than they are today. Whatever the causes, I think we must expect that Miss Hamlyn would be profoundly dispirited by what she could observe in 1983 as compared, say, with 1938, the last complete year of peace before the war.

I do not think we should allow ourselves the belief that either Parliament or the courts have gone soft on crime. On the contrary, although there are from time to time inevitably cases of excessive lenience, I believe that the vastly increased array of methods of penal treatment open to a sentencing judge is not only more humane, but also more efficient, than a régime of savage penalties and long custodial sentences. Contrary to some populist views hastily expressed, I do not favour an appeal in cases of excessive lenience at the court of trial. I believe adherence to the principle that no man should be twice put in jeopardy for the same offence applies equally to appeals against sentence alleged to be excessively lenient as to appeals against perverse acquittals. Both obviously take place. But the price is worth paying in each case. Equally I deprecate the somewhat rarer outbursts of public indignation against what are alleged to be excessively severe sentences. Where sentences are alleged to be too severe the arguments against them are better deployed calmly and rationally on appeal.

The provision of criminal legal aid on the scale on which it is now available, coupled with the rule that an acquitted defendant is, in general, entitled to reimbursement of his costs, constitutes of course a vast improvement on anything which existed before the war. I do not wish anyone to understand me in a contrary sense.

This does not, however, reduce what I have repeatedly said on the need to contain the costs of criminal legal aid and the need to impose some discipline on the use to which it is put, if not identical with, at least analogous to, that which works comparatively well in civil litigation. The test in each case is that the assisted litigant should be constrained to observe the disciplines which an unassisted litigant would reasonably be advised to accept both as to plea and evidence. The fact that I have not yet discovered a philosopher's stone in this regard (if any exists) does not diminish the conviction with which I say these things. Despite continuing efforts to contain it, criminal legal aid is still cascading out of control as the result of the lack of a suitable comprehensive structure of discipline operating on those who make use of it. An unassisted defendant is constrained by the discipline of the marginal utility of expenditures, and this discipline applies not only to plea, but to the conduct of a case generally. There is no less reason why similar constraints should not operate with equal force on assisted defendants and their advisers.

One of the results of the increased volume of criminal proceedings is delay. Compared with the period before the war, the delay in bringing criminal cases to trial, whether in summary cases or before the Crown Court, continues to give cause for concern. Delay both inflicts injustice and affects the quality of justice when the time of trial arises. Our system of justice depends for its efficiency on the recollection of witnesses examined orally, and this method of trial becomes less and less efficient as time passes and recollections fade and blur. Happily this does not, as a rule, impair the chances of the acquittal of defendants. In general this is taken care of by the burden of proof. But the prosecution is entitled to justice as much as the defence, and justice for the prosecution requires the conviction of the guilty on established proof, just as justice for the accused implies a quick release from anxiety, respect for his rights, a fair trial, and acquittal of the innocent.

It was, in fact, the congestion in the courts which led to the passing of the Courts Act in 1971. Despite some tooth sucking by traditionalists, this, in itself, has led to a vast improvement in the whole administration of criminal justice. But, by itself, it was not enough. A large additional provision of court accommodation has been required, and continues to be needed. The appointment under the legislation of a great number of deputy judges, assistant recorders, recorders, and judges has really revolutionised the effectiveness of the means at the disposal of Lord Chancellors for discerning the true judicial potential of candidates for appointment. The obligation on magistrates under the Act to sit with the Crown Court judge has, I believe, both improved their understanding of the nature of the criminal process and their relationship with the professional judiciary. During my first term as Lord Chancellor, I was able to reduce the average time between committal and arraignment (which is the critical statistic for trials on indictment) by half. But this was done by measures which cannot easily be repeated, namely the provision of new courts and the appointment of additional numbers of judges. During the succeeding five years delays crept up again, and, by 1979, had returned to the unacceptable level which I had found in 1970 and was still rising. This was due partly to the increase in business over the intervening years, and partly to the unfortunate fact, for which I can find no adequate justification, that, countrywide, contested trials on indictment are taking approximately two hours each longer to dispose of than they were 10 years ago. It takes a long time to stem the momentum of a movement of this kind, and 12 months after I took office in 1979 I was still struggling against a trend in the wrong direction, though this was by then beginning to diminish. I am happy to say that the tide seems to have turned and that the movement is now slightly in my favour. But it is too early as yet to express anything more than cautious optimism. There is no reasonable prospect of increasing the speed of the court building programme. In the years to come the increased numbers practising at the bar and as solicitors (the practising bar has approximately doubled over the last 10 years) can be expected to yield a satisfactory increase in the numbers of suitable candidates for judicial appointment. But, short of my making premature or unsuitable appointments, which I am not prepared to contemplate, this is a prospect only of gradual improvement in the availability of judicial manpower. In the immediate future more is to be gained in improved arrangements for pretrial co-operation and preparations, better listing (involving less waiting time), fewer applications for adjournment, the discouragement of frivolous applications for a change of adviser, and a more compendious style of advocacy and preparation. I am, I am bound to say, rather puzzled at certain related differences in performance between one part of the country and another. When I last enquired, I was informed that in London and the South East, where the delays are worst, only about 44 per cent. of those arraigned in the Crown Court pleaded guilty and that of the remaining 56 per cent. who pleaded not guilty, about 50 per cent. were acquitted. By contrast, of those arraigned in the North East about 76 per cent. pleaded guilty, although of the remaining 24 per cent. again about 50 per cent. were acquitted. The delays in the North East are about half what they are in the South East and London. Obviously these figures are significant. But what do they mean? Are they the product of delay or the cause of it or, as I suspect, both? Do they reflect differences in attitude or efficiency on the part of the prosecution in the two contrasted areas? Do they reflect differences in attitude by the juries and, if so, what is the cause of such differences? Is there any difference in the types of offence charged or committed? These are all questions to which I would like to know the answers. But, as I do not, I must pass on.

The relationship between the strictness of law enforcement at the street level by police and at the court level by the judiciary has obviously a direct bearing on the level of criminal activity. But the relationship is not, I believe, capable of analysis in crude terms. The most important factor is not, I am sure, so much the severity of individual sentences as the general level of detection, conviction, and the infliction, in the end, of a general level of adequate penalties. I do not, for instance, and to cite one notorious recent case, believe that

Law and Order

the infliction of a fine of £2,000 in a single case of rape would
encourage many people to commit that odious offence at that
price. On the other hand, the fact that the offence is known
normally to attract a substantial custodial sentence does, I
believe, play a substantial part in discouraging that sort of
crime and is in that sense a deterrent, not so much because the
thought enters much into the subjective motivation of individual offenders, but because it influences the general social
consciousness that such conduct is unacceptable, and held in
hatred by right minded people. It is important that all concerned with law enforcement from the police to the Court of
Appeal should bear some sort of relationship to the general
moral climate of opinion around them. If they disregard this
or find themselves wholly out of touch with it in their treatment of suspects or actual offenders—either in the direction
of lenience or severity—they are apt to produce violent reac-
tion against their conduct. They can hope to influence the
moral climate in either direction only so long as they take
account of it. They can lead it, but, save in the rarest
instances, they cannot wrench it, in the right direction.

The relationship between law and order and law enforcement is, however, less direct and more complicated than the
assumptions of my present remit allow me to explore. I am
sure that the incidence of criminal activity is not simply
capable of explanation in terms of institutions or structural
arrangements as the assumptions of a Hamlyn lecturer compel him to suppose. Rather, it is a function of the attitude of
the members of a society to moral standards and political
authority in general. Obviously if police or the courts are
either lax or unduly lenient or repressive or over-severe, law
and order will deteriorate, and in extreme cases relapse into
anarchy. But a society which allows itself to become doubtful
of the objective value of moral standards generally, or to

adopt a questioning or negative attitude towards political authority, will inevitably encourage political dissent or alienation to relapse into violence or other forms of lawlessness, and will encourage other behaviour of a more explicitly criminal nature. Any attempt to explain away the rising crime rate in terms of a single explanation, economic recession, the class system, the policy of governments, the exhibition on the media of violent, or sexually exciting, scenes, or plots implicitly condoning dishonesty, is bound to fall down. Conduct with good or bad social consequences cannot be categorised neatly into actions which are specifically criminal and those which are merely undesirable, or into those which clearly ought to be made mandatory and those which are merely regarded as praiseworthy. But a society which either seeks to deny the morally obligatory character of all right action or to adopt a purely positivist attitude to law and thus to remove from law its relationship to purely moral conceptions is, I would venture to think, certain to find itself in very grave trouble in law enforcement. This is perhaps only another way of asserting in rather more stilted language the second part of the language of Miss Hamlyn's request. But I would slightly rephrase it. Irrespective of the question whether our institutions make it a "privilege" to be British, but simply if we wish to make and keep it so, the need of the present day is less to expound the comparative excellence of our institutions than to urge the general obligation for all who wish to preserve or extend our blessings to recognise the necessity for promoting general moral standards, obeying such standards themselves, and adapting our institutions in such a way as to encourage willing conformity to them by all.

Conclusion

I have now come full circle. There is nothing in Miss Hamlyn's bequest which compels her lecturer to confine his message to legal topics. But tradition and your choice of lecturer have really prescribed that he should do so. The choice of myself as the thirty-fifth lecturer made it quite certain that my choice of topic should fall at the point at which law and politics share a common frontier.

What I have sought to do is to examine the terms of the bequest after a lapse of 40 years since the founder's decease and to consider in the light of what has happened since how far they can be faithfully observed in 1983. It now remains to consider the result.

Miss Hamlyn died in 1941 in the year which, as matters turned out, was the turning point in the war. 1941 had seen Hitler's crazy and treacherous attack on the Soviet Union, and the equally treacherous and equally foolish Japanese raid on Pearl Harbour. With America and Russia both involved on our side we could hardly lose in the end, and the threat of invasion lost reality. By 1942, the tide had turned. After Alamein Rommel was thrown out of Africa. Stalingrad held.

In Britain thoughts were beginning to turn to the post-war world which was to come. No single event directed them to this discussion more than the publication of the Beveridge Report.

It so happened that the same events precipitated a crisis in my own affairs. In the late summer of 1942 I was struck down by a severe attack of infective hepatitis and my health, which had hitherto been marked A1, was permanently degraded to the point at which it was apparent to me that I had no longer a useful military role to play. I decided to return to the House of Commons of which I had been an absent member for some two years. I think it was the publication of the Beveridge Report that helped me to make up my mind. When I got back I found that others of my contemporaries had almost simultaneously made the same decision. I have been continuously in public life throughout the period under consideration, and for the greater part of it I have been practising the law.

It is difficult to recapture the atmosphere of those days. In my own party I soon found then that I was thought to be a dangerous radical, a "young man in a hurry" as one of my Conservative colleagues, parodying Disraeli, put it. But, as the election of 1945 was to show, I was in truth far behind, and not in advance of, the radicalism of the country as a whole.

What I think was clear to me at the time was that if our political continuity was to be maintained a radical change in the system of social security was required. The Beveridge Report was the banner round which the younger Conservatives rallied. We neither foresaw nor desired the massive increase which followed in 1945 in what has now come to be called the public sector of industry. Our formula, so far as we could be said to have had one, was "publicly organised social service and privately owned industry." I do not think that any one of us would have been happy at the thought of a £130,000 million scale of annual expenditure, or the devotion of nearly half of our national income to fiscal revenue, local or central. I am sure that Miss Hamlyn would have been equally horrified.

I think, too, that neither she nor I foresaw or desired the terrible divides which now separate the world into East, West and the Third World. In 1942 all hoped that the terrible events of 1940 in the West and 1941 in the East would turn the two rival ideologies of Communism and democracy towards one another, and towards the making of a more stable, unified, and peaceful civilisation. I do not think that she or I would have foreseen or desired either the speed at which the British Empire was to be liquidated after 1948, nor the degree of alienation between its various parts which has followed its liquidation, and I am sure she would have been slow to approve the frantic desire for total independence and refusal to opt firmly for democracy in any intelligible sense which has since characterised most of the peoples for whose fate we had hitherto been responsible. Nor at that time did any of us foresee the rise of Israel as an independent nation state and the momentous consequences it has brought about in the Middle East.

All these are negative facts of which if he is to be honest with himself and his audience the thirty-fifth Hamlyn lecturer must take account when he sets himself the task of meeting Miss Hamlyn's wishes in 1983. It is idle to pretend that either law or legal institutions can exist in a social or political vacuum, and there are numerous factors which make our position less favourable than we had hoped.

Internally, there have been immense gains. Never before has the population of Britain been so well educated, so well insured against poverty or disease, and if not now fully employed, against the consequences of unemployment. Despite all talk of polarisation, never in my lifetime have

there been fewer class differences, fewer differences in standards of material well-being, than we have now, and, though
our economic efficiency has not shone in comparison with
others (a comparison Miss Hamlyn expressly invites me to
make), especially our former enemies, the totality of national
wealth, of individual incomes, or of social security benefits has
never been as high, and, in my judgment, barring external
catastrophe, it is likely to rise again over the years in the
future.

These factors have ensured the continuity of British life, its
constitutional arrangements, its laws, its liberties, and its
sense of nationhood. Though we live in a very different world
from that which was envisaged at the date of the trust, and one
in many ways much more dangerous and much less happy, it is
still a privilege to live in these islands, and to preserve our
essential values, institutions and customs, and to hand them
on to our children is still a duty and responsibility which we
should be proud to shoulder.

So far Miss Hamlyn's message is amply justified in both its
parts. I do not find anything in the essential structure of our
institutions or our law, or our sense of continuity with our
past, which I should wish to alter.

On the other hand we must remember that, however much
our absolute wealth may have increased, Britain continues to
pursue her destiny in conditions far less stable, less secure,
and less within our own power to control than ever before
since the reign of Elizabeth I. This is a fact of which lawyers
and statesmen must necessarily take account as we approach
the second millennium of the Christian era. Moreover, the
continuity of our tradition is sadly shaken by the absence of an
agreed set of values, moral, political, and spiritual, without
which no law or liberty can indefinitely survive. It is easy, and,
of course, within limits essential, to proclaim the sacred right

of uninhibited controversy. But, in my judgment at least, what this nation needs is ballast and cement, a renewed sense of unity and purpose, a revived recognition of objective moral principle and respect for authority. Unlike the laws of the Medes and Persians which can never be changed, the British legal tradition, under the able tutelage of the two Law Commissions and the constantly shifting currents of world events, is in a state of constant evolution and adjustment. That is a sign of health and life. But to exist at all law must have at least a certain durability. Authority and tradition demand more than a casual respect. A state which hopes to survive cannot persist indefinitely in a perpetual state of turmoil. Its institutions, its customs and traditions, its national personality must be seen to endure and maintain their identity in the midst of change. There is room for periods of quiescence and consolidation as well as for periods of growth and creativity. Having said which I trust that in 2018 (or thereabouts) Miss Hamlyn's seventieth lecturer will be preparing to deliver his own series of lectures. With that I take my leave.

Index